Craig McGregor

Pop Goes the Culture

Pluto Press

Parts of this book appeared in *Soundtrack for the Eighties*
published in 1983 by Hodder and Stoughton (Australia)
Pty Limited, 2 Apollo Place, Lane Cove, NSW 2066.

British edition, incorporating new material,
first published in 1984 by Pluto Press Limited,
The Works, 105a Torriano Avenue, London NW5 2RX

Cover designed by Clive Challis A. Gr. R.

Set by Grassroots, London NW6.
Printed in Great Britain by Photobooks Limited, Bristol

ISBN 0-86104-750-8

I would like to thank the Literature Board
of the Australia Council, and the Harkness
Fellowship, for their help in making this book possible.

Craig McGregor is one of Australia's leading writers and
cultural critics. He was born in Jamberoo, has lived in London, New York, San Francisco and Repentance Creek, and is
now back in Sydney. His previous books on popular culture
include *Bob Dylan: A Retrospective*; *This Surfing Life*; *People, Politics and Pop*; and *Up Against The Wall, America*. He
has written two novels, a rock opera, and several commen-
taries on Australia.

Contents

Everyone, finally, outside his or her professional activity, carries on some form of intellectual activity, that is, is a 'philosopher', an artist, possesses taste, participates in a particular conception of the world, has a conscious line of moral conduct, and therefore contributes to sustain a conception of the world or to modify it, that is, to bring into being new modes of thought.

Antonio Gramsci

Introduction

Like most rock critics, I'm actually a print addict. The only magazines I buy every week are *New Musical Express* (*NME*) and *City Limits* (for their information services), but for as long as I can remember I've had a weekly routine (shared by an increasing, jostling number of people)—Friday afternoon in Smiths, skimming through every vaguely cultural weekly. The rest of the music papers, *New Society* and *New Statesman*, the *Times Supplements*, *Time Out*, the *Listener* and *Time* and *Newsweek*. The same pattern for the monthlies: I buy the *Face* but speed-read all the hi-fi and musician magazines, too, keep an eye out for the new *Smash Hits*, *New Socialist*, *Marxism Today*, *Harpers and Queen*, for Penny Valentine's column in *19*, Ian Birch's pop page in *Company*. What I'm really addicted to is cultural commentary.

Craig McGregor is a cultural commentator and a fascinating one just because he doesn't write for the magazines I normally read. He's Australian, but this matters less for what he writes about (entertainment is multinational, the USA is hegemonic in pop terms), than for the context in which his arguments work. The starting-point for all pop criticism must be that pop is a culture of consumption—we're dealing with commodities. McGregor's point is that the idea of passive consumption is misleading. Pop critics are employed as consumer guides, intervening in the marketplace. Their task is to persuade people to consume in certain ways, for specific reasons. Consumption is an ideological act. Consumers themselves have a stake in the process of interpretation, argument, making sense—which is why other people's reviews are so compulsively irritating, why music papers' record and concert critiques get the most passionate reader-response. Consumption, market choice, is also an issue of aesthetic choice, cultural judgement—even the most 'mindless' consumer invests in an argument.

One reason, then, why I read all those magazines (and listen faithfully to Radio 1's *Round Table*) is to follow the arguments, to keep tabs on the ways in which popular cultural meanings are made. The print media still have the most important interpretative role in consumption, still have a determinant effect on the shape of popular culture, on its class structure, its hierarchy of values, its distribution of symbolic capital and power. The final political significance of cultural icons—Boy George, *Gandhi*, *The Boys from the Blackstuff*—is an effect of all the judgements passed on them (as *Titbits* and the *New Statesman* explain what Boy George's sex life really means, as *Socialist Worker* and the *Sun* and *Screen* spell out the message of Yosser Hughes). Pop culture can't exist without such running commentary.

Still, pop opinion can be more or less enlightening, and at the moment cultural commentators in Britain are decidedly dull—it's easy enough to guess what opinions everyone's going to have about everything; criticism has become a matter of confirming prejudice. Pop commentary should be a mode of exploration, discovery, opening up meanings (as in the best British work of, say, Orwell or Colin MacInnes or George Melly) but these days the dominant mood is the opposite—criticism means closing down sense, slotting goods and styles into established frameworks. There are exceptions, of course, writers or pieces that startle by their refusal to be bound by a line. Still, the use of a personal voice (I'm thinking of C.L.R. James's cricket pieces in *Race Today*, Penny Reel's occasional autobiographical pop notes in *NME*) comes across as oddly naive amidst the routine impersonality of most other writers. I once had the idea of gathering all the articles I'd clipped from the music press and bringing them out in book form—say, *The Best of British Rock Writing*—but reading the pieces again, out of their news context, they suddenly seemed feeble, without presence, unable to carry anything but topical weight. Naivety, it now seems clear to me, is a more solid quality than knowingness. It is a greater tribute to McGregor's work than it may seem to say that it is so readable as a book.

There are obvious reasons why pop-cultural commentary in Britain is inadequate. Most simply, there's the problem of space. Certainly in the mainstream press (I'm talking from *Sunday Times* experience) pop critics are given no room to make an argument (as opposed to a summary opinion), and certainly no room to develop that argument, to doubt or debate. Even in the music papers (which, if anything, give their writers too much room) the pressure of pop as news, the constant competition to anticipate the new thing first, means that instant categorisation has to be the critical norm. *NME's* writers, for example, seem to lose interest in acts or musics precisely at the moment when they are beginning to have their popular effects. And then there's the problem of critical personality— original critics become trapped by their originality, as stars themselves, so that writers as different from each other as Peter York, Julie Burchill and Keith Waterhouse—all of whom once had important suggestions to make about the effects of popular culture—now write increasingly as parodies of themselves, bound by their by-lines.

But the limitations of current British pop commentary aren't just a matter of space and time and personality. There are wider ideological issues involved, which are put into perspective by McGregor's Aussie assumptions. When I first read his pieces I was, by turn, interested, moved, instructed and annoyed. What most struck me, though, was a tone of voice that's unusual in British pop criticism—a tone of doubt, openness, space, hesitation. Even more noticeable, the second time through, was a mood of friendly, urgent persuasion: McGregor writes as if he doesn't expect readers immediately to agree with him. This is even more unusual. My most regular sources of cultural opinion, *NME* and *City Limits*, are both (in different ways and with different jargon) over-sure of themselves, shameless in proclaiming 'correct' views, bland in their assumptions that their readers share their views, that anyone who doesn't is automatically excluded from the discussions that matter.

There are, I think, a number of reasons why British approaches to popular culture seem so restricted. First, then, it is striking how deeply the traditional high culture/low culture division (which McGregor addresses) still plagues our cultural common sense. The obvious sign of this is the amount of attention that continues to be devoted to traditional bourgeois art forms even in leftish magazines like the *New Statesman*, in 'mass' media like radio and television. What's taken for granted on most arts pages is that 'high' cultural forms (opera, for example) should be approached with an intellectural seriousness that's inappropriate to low cultural forms, to 'entertainment'.

This has had a number of consequences. There's still a tendency, for example, to justify the 'serious' treatment of a pop commodity by first redescribing it in art terms—this happened to rock in the mid-1960s as it had happened to film in the 1930s. This approach marks the treatment of 'pop' items on TV arts programmes such as the *South Bank Show*. Alternatively, and equally unhelpfully, pop culture is treated as a sociological curio, in what I think of as the *New Society* approach (and my own, to some extent): pop is described lovingly enough, but it is not engaged with. Even within pop practice itself the spectre of high culture lurks. It's reflected in a recurrent coolness of critical tone, in the emphasis on irony, in an implicit suggestion that 'pop doesn't really matter' (not in the way, as bourgeois critics take for granted, that Beethoven really matters). There's a defensiveness about pop seriousness—in short, a terror of pretension and pseudery. Such caution is not surprising because so much serious writing on pop *is* pretentious, *does* claim value for pop in quite ludicrous high-cultural terms.

Precisely because there isn't a flourishing tradition of serious pop criticism, writers have too often had to take their aesthetic terms from elsewhere. (It's interesting to compare the situation in the USA, where magazines like *Village Voice* and the early *Rolling Stone* took pop seriously enough to allow critics— Greil Marcus, Bob Christgau and Dave Marsh, for instance— to develop an *aggressive* rock aesthetic.)

There are further considerations, too. Take the issue of class. In Britain it's taken for granted (on the left as well as on the right) that high/low, art/pop distinctions reflect class divisions—high art means bourgeois art; low art, mass culture, is produced for and consumed by the working class. Popular culture has a far more complicated structure than this, as is obvious in the Australian context, where high culture, European-style, is in a sense an 'alien' form. 'Australian culture' is, by self-proclamation, a 'classless' mass culture, a form of nationalism—hence its value and all our Aussie jokes (read Craig McGregor on Barry Humphries). The same argument can obviously be made about the USA—Ronald Reagan is not exactly a high cultural figure; it has relevance for Britain, too—mass culture, whether in the form of pop music, the popular press, cinema or television, is as important for the making of the middle class (perhaps more important) as for the making of the working class. To put it another way, we can't ('we' meaning intellectuals, writers, journalists, teachers, *experts*) simply write about popular culture as if it is something that happens to other people.

This point lies at the centre of McGregor's approach. The most debilitating effect of high-art assumptions about culture has been to define it in terms of objects, events, texts (literary criticism remains the model for all cultural analysis) rather than in terms of activities, processes, practice. British cultural theorists are thus experts in ideology, in *after-the-event* cultural readings; at the same time, they are remarkably uninterested in cultural predictions, in tracing audience-response. Who would have guessed, for example, from reading all those cultural commentators that Britain would become the world's heaviest users of home videos? Who now knows what this means? As McGregor argues, cultural value lies in *activity*. Maybe the touchstone for pop criticism should not be art (with its assumptions about the artist, the audience, the aura, and so on) but sports and hobbies, dances and parties, fashion and decoration, collective acts of creation. Just as pop fanzines capture the *enthusiasm* of consumption (an aspect that always evades professionals), so one startling effect of the new teenage magazine *17* (from the *Smash Hits* stable) lies in its imitation of the fashion fanzine *i-D*. Instead of parading a house model for its readers, *17* takes pictures of people on the streets, asks them how they came to dress that way, defines teen-style as a matter of active consumption.

If the high/low culture distinction runs through the British media like a watermark, so does sectarianism. Much pop criticism is taken up with building (or destroying) cults and sects and myths; a record, a musician, a genre is either in or out, correct or incorrect. In the music papers the bickering about particular acts is just silly, but in the radical press the urge to certainty has more damaging effects. The constant attempt to put music in its place—a place defined by its contribution to a predefined position on class or race or sex—conceals the fact that pop culture, like everything else, is riddled with contradictions. The task of cultural commentary is to unravel the contradictions, to intervene in the fight for meaning, to learn from cultural experience; it is not to squeeze all events into a prefigured political shape. The latter strategy condemns us to a trailing role, running along behind cultural developments, awarding medals and brickbats long after the time when such judgements can have any effect. Pop culture reveals how capitalist ideology *works* (and how hard it has to work); the point of cultural commentary is to point to the problems commodities conceal, not to pretend that if music isn't properly proletarian it isn't 'worth' anything.

Writing this, my head suddenly filled with half-remembered debates about realism, the commodity form, the construction of desire, I'm aware of the final strand of British cultural analysis that McGregor exposes—its domination by the academy. In the last twenty years British cultural theory on the left has been plagued by a peculiarly arid form of intellectualism. The problem is not the development of a theoretical approach to culture as such (after all, the new gurus, Gramsci and Brecht, for example, are old left activists) but, rather, the *inwardness* of the arguments (I'm thinking of the debates about structuralism, representation, psychoanalysis)—their terms and references and assumptions can only be understood within the right framework, they're meaningless outside it.

The result is another form of cult-building, another example of critical judgements made to exclude those not in the know—so that, bizarrely, the people are excluded from accounts of popular culture. All the excluded can do is fall back on a defensive ignorance—'I know what I like ...' The problem, in short, is to translate the claims of structuralism, or whatever, into the terms of popular culture *in order to test them*. This has rarely been done in Britain because of the huge gap between the smug middlebrow assumptions of the 'quality' press and the

the academic introversion of cultural radicals. I've always thought, for example, that someone like Dick Hebdige should have a weekly cultural column in the *Guardian*. This would certainly be one strategy for applying criticism—theory as entertainment (the strategy flourished briefly in *NME* in the person of the over-playful Ian Penman).

McGregor's strategy is rather different—he offers theory in an earnest spirit, and thus opens himself up to the charge of intellectual directness, which, for both the cool ironists of the pop press and the discourse theorists of the academic press, seems to be a sin. What neither group realises is how refreshing it is to read someone responding to culture without first proclaiming his detachment. What McGregor offers, above all, is a sense of cultural engagement. This partly emerges from his autobiographical presence. British pop criticism veers between presenting critics as stars—extra-sensitively perceptive—or concealing their personal habits altogether. What we lack is an understanding of criticism as itself a popular cultural practice, an attempt to make sense of a life, the critic's, with the same pop tools as the rest of us use. To read McGregor's thoughts on growing up in Australia, his moving account of the USA in the early 1970s, is to be reminded how few autobiographical accounts we've got of growing up in Britain since rock 'n' roll. Both the women's and the gay movements have recognised the role of autobiography in the development of political theory (this is an aspect of the collapsing distinction between the personal and the political). The insight should be applied to cultural theory generally.

As it is, McGregor's self-reflections reveal powerfully how muddled our experiences of pop have been. Central to his story is the brooding presence of the USA itself. It is a truism that popular culture is dominated by US capital, but the glib anti-Americanism current in both the left and the pop press evades the fact that our dreams and desires have been Americanised whether we like it or not, and that American dreams give shape to quite contrary urges, articulate the promise (as well as the lie) of abundance. It is easy enough to dismiss as fantasy US accounts of happiness and equality, but such fantasies are at the heart of all revolutionary utopianism; US culture, far more clearly than British culture, values participation, community action, self-determination. McGregor describes wonderfully well the *exhilaration* of American popular culture, the myth of space and movement that is 'real', as a myth, even for the USA's most oppressed, exploited people—why else did jazz and blues, do rap and salsa, carry such an emotional charge?

The USA, in this context, stands for capitalism—it is capital that has a built-in urge to disrupt the world, to disorder people's lives in ways that contradict its ideological calls for order, stability, firmness. There's a kind of orthodoxy in left cultural thinking that dismisses all pop as essentially conservative, positing order, confirming the way things are. Radical culture, it seems, should celebrate disorder, art should make people unsure. McGregor suggests another possibility. Capitalism's real effects (removing jobs, shoving people round labour markets, breaking up communities, changing ideas to suit profits) mean that popular culture becomes a way (the only way?) of seizing order from the ruins, making sense where there is none, hanging on to hope. McGregor is, of course, a hippie-influenced dreamer, someone for us to scoff at. But reading his book, I found myself trusting his memory. Counterculture did matter. Still does.

Simon Frith

Jazz

1. Jazz: Starting to Think

The first music I ever heard that was remotely like jazz was George Gershwin's *Rhapsody in Blue*. It was a rainy Saturday evening, I was a boarder at Cranbrook school, and in desperation the masters (as they were, and still are, called) took us down to the Double Bay Vogue to see Oscar Levant play and act his way through Gershwin's life story. When, towards the climax of the film, I heard that long, rising clarinet glissando which opens *Rhapsody in Blue* I felt a real sense of excitement, of quite unpremeditated exhilaration, of the sort which I was familiar with from reading literature but not from listening to music. Though I didn't realise it at the time, I was responding to my first experience of blues tonalities, idioms and expressions, albeit transmuted by Gershwin's white/Jewish sensibility, and I have been deeply involved in the blues, and jazz, and the musics which spring from them, ever since.

It wasn't long after that initiation that I found myself listening to some swing records which one of the boarders had brought to school. 'It's jazz,' he said, and played Tommy Dorsey, Glenn Miller, Artie Shaw. It wasn't, and I didn't like it much. If this was jazz, it wasn't for me. And there it might all have ended had not some other students got together and, under the aegis of our history teacher, Harry Nicolson, formed a jazz club. As a barely tolerated junior I heard classic New Orleans jazz for the first time: Bunk Johnson, Jelly Roll Morton, Johnny Dodds, Kid Ory, Louis Armstrong. I still couldn't make sense of it. Bunk Johnson's shouting, collective improvisation was far too complex and apparently undisciplined for me to grab hold of; I couldn't decipher the themes, or what each instrument was doing, or what the basic structure of the music was. It wasn't until I heard Bessie Smith's blues, with jazz instrumentalists such as Armstrong and Joe Smith and Clarence Williams accompanying her, that I began to understand what was happening; and, understanding, to react fully to the amazing artistic experience of jazz. That led me back, eventually, to the black country blues (at Palings I picked up Melodisc singles by weirdly named singers I had never heard of: Muddy Waters? Leadbelly? John Lee Hooker?), and spirituals, and the immense reservoir of Afro-American folk music (posing as secretary of the jazz club, I borrowed the Library of Congress recordings from the U.S. Embassy), and then forward again through boogie woogie, ragtime, dixieland, bop, modern jazz, 'the new thing', gospel, soul, rhythm and blues and rock 'n' roll: nearly all of them created by black Americans in one astonishing and sustained outpouring of creativity. But jazz was at the centre of it; and it was by listening to jazz, talking about it, discussing it with my brothers, playing Melodiscs and Parlophones and Deccas on a beat-up wind-up gramophone converted to Electric Reproduction, going to the Sydney Jazz Club, listening to Eric Child and Ron Wills and the A.B.C., reading *Downbeat* and imported English jazz magazines and jazz writers such as Rudi Blesh and Charles Delauney and Charles Edward Smith, that I learned to think.

For myself.

Hard to explain that, really. But learning doesn't take place in a vacuum; it has to fasten onto something, something substantial, a subject, a theme, perhaps a discipline or art form or subject area which the learner responds to intuitively but doesn't understand intellectually, and for me it was jazz. Because, somehow or other, by thinking about jazz as well as listening to it I began to connect things together for the first time, to make jumps between things which seemed quite unrelated; I began to understand something about the nature of art, and its likely modes of development, and the relationship between art and society. In a way I was fortunate to have been given something like jazz to start with, because jazz presents, in compressed form, a perfect example of the trajectory described by most art forms in the course of their evolution, from folk origins, through archaic, classic, and expressionist forms, to fragmentation and (possibly) disintegration. In the progress from Mississippi cottonfield arwhoolies, to Louis Armstrong's opening trumpet solo on 'Wild Man Blues', to Albert Ayler's dying testament to the agony yet triumph of twentieth-century man, the history of art.

All art springs, as I will argue later, from folk or popular sources. Its characteristics at this stage tend to be communality, spontaneity (improvisation), and an emphasis on intensity of expression rather than formality of mode. This was certainly the case with the Afro-American folk music forms that were the forerunners of jazz: blues, spirituals, work songs, children's song, arwhoolies, jigs and dances, shouts, hollers and ballads. Much of this music was functional, and when 'jass' bands evolved in New Orleans at the turn of the century, their music retained this functionality: for dancing, marching, or funerals. But as jazz became more and more a music for entertainment, so it began to be transformed into an *art* music; the marching brass bands of New Orleans, such as the Eureka Brass Band, and the bands of musicians such as Buddy Bolden and Bunk Johnson were already playing archaic jazz—archaic in the sense that it was an art at the very start of a long line of development. Like Greek sculpture at a similar stage of evolution, it displayed what have come to be regarded as the typical qualities of archaic art: a certain rigidity of expression; a clear and manifest sense of tradition; and an increasing exploration of formal values. It's interesting that some of the bands of the English and Australian traditional jazz revival of the 1960s returned quite deliberately to this pre-classic form of jazz; Ken Colyer's and Geoff Bull's bands carefully imitated the collective sound and archaic tonalities of the George Lewis and Kid Howard groups, and their leaders made ritual pilgrimages back to New Orleans to try to discover how the 'real' jazz sounded before the classicists like Louis Armstrong got hold of it. In some ways this seems a bizarre attitude, but you only have to listen to the music to have it explained; there is a certain uncompromising power to archaic jazz, just as there is to Greek sculpture of the seventh and sixth centuries B.C., which is impressive in its own right. The same applies to folk art forms; whereas they might once have been dismissed as primitive or undeveloped, we have come to appreciate their innate and formidable artistic qualities. This is so obvious that the feuds and schisms which spring up between different schools of jazz devotees seem incomprehensible; when I was growing up, the big feud was between boppers and mouldie fygges, but I suppose that sort of infighting is a sign of vitality, if nothing else!

The archaic period in Greek sculpture lasted perhaps 200 years, the archaic period in jazz about twenty. By the time jazz had travelled out of New Orleans and through the southern and border-north states to Chicago, it had been expanded, developed and formalised to the point where it can be described as 'classic' and it had, of course, displayed the sort of profound artistic achievement we associate with classicism. The basic jazz band formula had been fixed: a three-instrument front line consisting of trumpet (or cornet), trombone and clarinet, with the trumpet taking the lead and the others improvising in response, plus a three- or four-person rhythm section consisting of drums, banjo, bass and possibly piano. It was a communal music of collective improvisation still, in which everyone had a part to play and hardly anyone stood out from the others. There were few solos, the band played chorus after chorus with everyone improvising on the theme together, and there were very few arrangements except 'head' arrangements (worked out in the head instead of being written down). Sometimes there might be a blues singer or vocalist with the group, but it was the *group* which counted and the music sounded very *together*. There was a balance, sometimes precarious, which again we associate with classicism in virtually all arts; a sense of thoroughly developed and worked-out limits within which an immense range of artistic creation was possible, so that at this stage the forms did not seem irksome (as they were to become) but rather provided a structure within which the artist could work with unimpaired freedom. The early King Oliver band, with Louis Armstrong playing second cornet, is a perfect example of this; there is almost a 'hurdy gurdy' sound to some of their performances, which is partly due to primitive recording techniques but also to this sense of perfect balance within a group framework. The basic problems of the form appear to have been solved, the limits defined and the art capable of infinite variation within those limits. In the 1920s, jazz reached a peak of development in the hands of gifted artists such as Oliver, Jelly Roll Morton, Sidney Bechet, Johnny Dodds, Louis Armstrong and many others, that established the form of classic jazz once and for all.

Classicism implies a certainty of form which is capable of revival. When the traditional jazz revival occurred, most of the bands, though not all, turned to classic jazz models. The San Francisco bands of Lu Watters and Turk Murphy, Australian bands such as Graeme Bell's and Frank Johnson's, and innumerable English bands consciously revived the techniques and sound of the classic era. The first jazz record I ever bought was by a group of precisely that nature: the Southern Jazz Group, an Adelaide band which Ron Wills had recorded on his own label and released on transparent blue vinyl! (Later my brother and I hitch-hiked down to Melbourne, which was the centre of the trad jazz revival, and spent just an hour ransacking the local record stores, before hitching straight back to Sydney with a pile of Bells, Barnards, Johnsons, Dave Dallwitzes and Tom Pickerings.) A parallel recreation of classicism occurred, strangely enough, with the black New Orleans artists who were rediscovered by American record collectors in the 1940s and who subsequently set off on new musical careers, as though the Depression years of working as storemen and packers, service station hands and cotton pickers, had never existed. Bunk Johnson's New Orleans Jazz Band, which included such musicians as George Lewis, Jim Robinson, Lawrence Marrero, Alcide Pavageau and Alton Purnell, played some of the most exhilarating classic jazz ever recorded. If you listen to their performances of 'Darktown Strutters Ball', 'When the Saints Go Marchin' In', 'Snag It' and 'High Society', the complexity, rhythmic drive and sheer hotness are phenomenal. I know of no greater demonstration of the virtues of classicism.

Classicism also implies revolution. The very stability of the form, which allows great art to be created, eventually becomes restrictive. The limits which were once supportive come to be seen as barriers. Artists begin experimenting with the forms, distorting them in order to achieve greater personal freedom in their work. The process is seen at its clearest in the work of Louis Armstrong, one of the true geniuses of jazz. Armstrong was born in New Orleans and was young enough to hear trumpeters like Bunk Johnson in their early days; he travelled to Chicago, joined King Oliver and for years played within the clear group limits of that band. But when Louis formed his own band, his music changed. In his early Hot Five recordings, the group sound remains fairly intact, despite Armstrong's increasing virtuosity as a horn player—a virtuosity that, in itself, presaged the breakdown of the traditional New Orleans collective ensemble. With his second Hot Five recordings, and of course his Hot Seven, he began playing long, highly developed solos which exploded out of (and exploded) the old conventions; the searing intensity of his solo on 'Wild Man Blues', its individuality, its technical display, and above all its sense of irresistible, vaulting imagination, meant that jazz had changed utterly. Even the group choruses sound different, with Louis dominating the others and fracturing the precious ensemble sound.

Now, whether one approves of or responds to this change in the nature of an established art form depends very much upon one's personal (and cultural) sensibility. There are critics and music lovers for whom classicism is everything, and for whom everything post-classic is a slow slide into degeneracy. As a boy, listening to jazz records in a tiny back bedroom, trying to work it out for myself—and driving the neighbours crazy—I at first resisted the direction jazz seemed to have taken in the late 1920s and, in a sense, was retaking as the trad jazz revival gathered momentum. The same remorseless logic of development seemed to be occurring, and bands that began as white New Orleans imitators rapidly evolved into Chicago-style groups of soloists and instrumentalists; the career of Bob Barnard, one of the finest jazz trumpeters in Australia, is a perfect example. With the puritanism of youth, I rejected all solo playing and set arrangements, and insisted on the integrity of collective group improvisation. Rudi Blesh, the American jazz critic and author of *Shining Trumpets*, was my mentor, and Leonard Feather a rat fink revisionist. But, after a time, I came to realise that the change was inevitable. Artists and art forms perform an almost predictable ritual of evolution; the individual listener may choose to tune into a certain stage to which his sensibility responds, and prefer Bach to Bartok or Johnny Dodds to Duke Ellington, but the art form itself never stands still.

By the 1930s Armstrong and others had pushed jazz into its expressionist phase. The change is from the group to the individual, from the collective sound to the solo, from improvisation to arrangement and, crucially, from classic self-restraint to post-classic self-expression. As in other arts, the forms are smashed to allow the individual artist as much freedom of expression as he demands. According to accounts of Armstrong's stage performances at this time, he was playing unprecedentedly long solo improvisations which lasted for ten minutes or more, creating ever more extended variations on a single theme. Recording technology, unfortunately, was still limited to the three-minute 78 r.p.m. disc, but if you listen to Armstrong's long, climactic solo on 'Tight Like That', with its carefully structured cadences and absolute dominance of the accompanying music, you get some idea of what he must have sounded like 'live'.

It wasn't only the instrumentalists who demanded preeminence for their own individual creativity; some arrangers did, too. Jelly Roll Morton was perhaps the first of the New Orleans bandleaders to demand that his musicians 'play it like he wrote it'. A comparison of the various takes of numbers like 'The Chant' and 'Dead Man Blues' reveals that these pieces were already fairly highly arranged, despite the freedom that Morton allowed his players during their solo breaks. Duke Ellington took it all a stage further, writing increasingly complex arrangements in which the old ideal of improvised music virtually disappeared and the ego dominance of the arranger was firmly established (I never liked Ellington much, and still don't, though I've come to respond to some of his major compositions: 'Take The A Train', 'Black, Brown and Beige', 'Minnie the Moocher'). Some of jazz's revolutionary qualities—the fusing of creation and performance, the 'hot' concept, the emphasis on blues tonalities and melodic invention instead of harmonic structure—faded away as jazz grew closer in concept to European art music.

In the late 1930s and early 1940s, therefore, jazz moved into the phase that almost invariably follows any expressionist era: fragmentation. Expressionism allows the artist to jump off in any direction whatsoever and, though there may for a while appear to be a mainstream, there are so many different artists with so many different ideas that the art form seems to move off in a chaotic variety of directions. The parallel with the development of expressionist theory and practice in twentieth-century European painting, and its subsequent multiplicity of movements, is fairly close. In the case of jazz it moved into big bands (Duke Ellington), swing (Count Basie, Benny Goodman), small combos (Lionel Hampton), post-blues torch songs (Ethel Waters, Billie Holiday), revivalism (Mezz Mezzrow, Kid Ory) and plain pop (Peggy Lee). There was a great deal of energy, and some remarkable recordings, and important advances in instrumental and arranging technique. But it wasn't a good time. The Depression forced a lot of jazzmen into retirement, or other jobs, or the commercial swing bands, and white bands and the white media took over and distorted to their own ends the music which had been created by black musicians, thus demonstrating both the racism and the corrupting commercialism of American society. The profoundly innovative thrust of jazz seemed to have ended up in the bland milk-and-water productions of hit parade bands such as Glenn Miller's.

Rescue was at hand. The idea of a mainstream in jazz or any other art form (*pace* Clement Greenberg) is an arguable one, especially if it is used to apply a set of criteria and critical imperatives to a rapidly evolving discipline, but many jazz musicians at the time felt there was a mainstream, and they didn't like it. Mainstream jazz was where it wasn't at. Most jazzmen were members of big bands, where they felt confined and unable to play what they wanted, so they began hanging out in after-hours nighteries such as Minton's in New York and playing together in impromptu jam sessions. These were self-conscious musical revolutionaries, and they included Charlie Parker, Thelonious Monk, Dizzy Gillespie, Bud Powell and Charlie Christian; they broke deliberately with the jazz tradition as it had been handed on to them and thus created, for the first time in jazz history, the notion of an avant-garde. They broke down the traditional harmonic structure of jazz, substituting a series of extravagant improvisations based on a skeletal chord structure, and developed new techniques, new tonalities and new concepts of what a mid-twentieth-century music should be. To the uninitiated it often sounded like a music of savage neurosis and alienation.

Writes Wilfrid Mellers in *Music in a New Found Land*:

"It was not an accident that modern jazz evolved during and in the wake of the Second World War, in which the Negro had been forced to fight to defend a freedom that seemed dubiously applicable to himself . . . A highly neurotic art, as symptom of a highly neurotic civilisation, cannot, however, be unexpected and may be valuable . . . For, despite the incidental affectations, the best modern jazz preserves the integrity of the great days of jazz history; the dedicated players would not compromise, even though Ellington had shown that compromise was possible. Rather than compromise, they were prepared to accept madness or death; and although this statement may sound melodramatic it is strictly true. As long as they could, they would create a chamber music—even a soloist's music—of protest and rejection, playing for themselves as Outsiders. They would accept the fact that the only vitality they could encompass was the nervous frenzy of a jungle turned to asphalt. Their music was their religion in that they put into it all the skeletonic truth they knew. Having played it, they died of consumption, drinks, drugs or mental breakdown."

As happens with any significant avant-garde movement, however, it was not long before the rest of the artistic community caught up with it. Today's avant-garde, whether created by a Picasso, or a Stravinsky or a Charlie Parker, is tomorrow's common ground. Bop created the essential structure of modern jazz and provided the basis for most contemporary movements in jazz; what followed the bop upheaval was another period of consolidation, refinement and differentiation. Miles Davis, for instance, began as a bop musician playing alongside Charlie Parker, but went on to become one of the founders of the 'cool' school in modern jazz, a movement which turned away from the high-strung intensity of bop towards a much mellower sound. Many of its players were white and tended towards a more conventional European tonality. There was also a conscious move by some jazzmen towards European chamber music. They were often highly educated, conservatory-trained musicians who attempted to bridge the gulf between jazz and 'classical' European music: hence third stream music, white groups such as Dave Brubeck's and black groups such as the Modern Jazz Quartet. Varieties of exoticism; at a time when traditions are breaking down, borrowings multiply and the eclectic creeps in. This in itself produced its own reaction in the form of a move by other jazz musicians to 'get back to the roots', which meant a return to blues sonorities, improvisation, and what came to be called funk.

A further development, in the 1970s, was the emergence of a new 'free form' jazz which dispensed with many of the limitations that even bop observed. The people who played it, as I explain in the essay 'Pop Goes The Culture', were not only musical revolutionaries but political revolutionaries, and you can hear it in their music; there is something infinitely moving about Albert Ayler's turmoiled, defiant outpouring, a spirit that is as intense and yet occasionally as lyrical as Louis Armstrong's forty years earlier. I first heard Albert Ayler, on record, in a Kings Cross flat when Horst Leipold, the jazz *aficionado* and promoter, started playing him after a late-night party. He played some Archie Shepp as well, but it was Ayler who caught me. I was as puzzled and yet as entangled as I had been when I first heard Bunk Johnson at the Cranbrook school Jazz Club. I bought whatever Ayler records I could and when, a few years later, my family and I went off to live in New York for two years, I was determined to catch up with him. I heard him once, late at night, on WABC, the black Harlem FM station, playing his superb 'Message from Albert': it always reminds me of Lennie Tristano's elegy for Charlie Parker, 'Requiem', in its unbearable conjunction of pathos and triumph. But just three months after we got to New York, I picked up a copy of the *New York Times* and suddenly read that the body of Albert Ayler, saxophonist, had been fished out of the East River the night before. He had been murdered; the talk among jazz musicians was that he had failed to deliver for some of the pushers who were running drugs down Manhattan's East Side. R.I.P., Albert.

These days jazz displays the sort of rich diversity that you would expect of a mature, highly developed art. If I had to summarise and simplify what I have been saying about the path described by most art forms it would be something like this: the trajectory is from folk or popular origins, to archaic forms, to classicism, to expressionism, to fragmentation; then, out of that fragmentation, the emergence of concepts such as mainstream and avant-garde, and the movements (rightly or wrongly) associated with them; and, subsequently, the development of an art characterised by complexity, and multiformity, and conflict.

I realise that this is an overly schematic and simplified model. All art is affected by the nature of the artists who create it and the character of the societies that produce it; the form achieved by any art at any stage of its development is the result of a complex amalgam of history, personality and social structure. But art grows, in part at least, from art, and art forms develop an evolutionary momentum of their own; otherwise it would be hard to explain what we mean by a 'tradition'. Even the most self-conscious revolutionaries come, in a sense, as fulfilments of existing traditions rather than instigators of new ones. Shakespeare, Picasso and John Coltrane can all be seen as the logical culminations of existing movements; none of them is explicable except in terms of what went before. The schema I have outlined can be applied, with equal validity, to such disparate art forms as Greek sculpture (pre-Hellenic to late Hellenistic), the film, and jazz; indeed, it is from Greek art that most of the terms are borrowed, and it was studying the bronze and marble forms of Greek sculpture in Athens, Delphi, Olympia, Corinth and Paris that first crystallised for me a real sense of what the terms meant. In comparatively new art forms, the successive stages of development are clear; that's especially the case if the changes are occurring in our own time, so that we are both witnesses to and involved in them. At each stage in the development of jazz, for instance, the music has reached such a point of refinement that it is capable of enduring as a sub-school on the contemporary scene, so that today we can still hear 'live' trad jazz and big band jazz, just as baroque and *lieder* are still performed on the world's concert stages; at the same time, the real action is elsewhere. Jazz is still evolving. Every now and then critics pronounce it dead, just as they pronounce the novel dead, but they are usually unaware of what is happening. The last time jazz was given its death rites by the ofays of the Western world, a revolutionary new form was cooking in the ghettos of New York, Newark and Oakland; the same is probably happening now. The miracle, not of perpetual motion, but of perpetual creation.

As I hope this essay makes clear, I personally owe a great debt to the generations of black artists who, hounded by racism and commercialism and exploitation, still managed to create one of the enduring art forms of our time. (So does the world.) They made me try to make my own music; I mean, you can hardly listen to jazz without wanting to perform the same bit of magic. (I can now play guitar and blues piano—badly.) Like all great art, it acts as an invitation to creation. More important, in my case, jazz acted as a focus for me as I grew up. It gave me many of the ideas I've been grappling with ever since: about art, and society, and culture, and how all ordinary people (i.e., *the people*) have greatness within them. Jazz made me understand how art is not the creation of single, isolated individuals but of communities, how culture means not artefacts, but activity, how tradition means not the dead weight of the past, but something dynamic and created anew by all those involved in it; and how everyone, players and listeners, writers and readers, actors and enactors, are all, finally, creators. They are joined in some sacred dance which requires everyone to participate; that's how art is, and what politics should be. For better or worse, and though they hardly intended it, those jazzmen scratching immortality into their 78 r.p.m. record grooves also taught an uncomprehending white Oz boy, growing up in a provincial city on the other side of the world, who had never heard the words 'racism', or 'communality', or even 'hot', to think.

(I think.)

1982

2. Lament for Louis

Louis Armstrong is dead. By now the rightful eulogies have been written. I don't need to add my own. Along with one or two other jazzman, such as Charlie Parker, he stands in a lonely pre-eminence. We all know that.

What we don't always remember is that in many ways Armstrong is a tragic figure, and his tragedy is part of larger one in which we all share. At first it doesn't seem so. Unlike Charlie Parker, John Coltrane, Buddy Bolden, Bix Beiderbecke, Charlie Christian, Albert Ayler—and the list seems endless—he made it through to old age. There was a resilience about Armstrong, a capacity to adapt his art to the time, which saw him through while others stumbled, buckled under pressure, died early and ignoble deaths.

But there's the rub. Armstrong survived by compromise, and it was a compromise which destroyed his art. It should never have been necessary, and unless we learn from his fate how commercialism can corrode even a creative artist of genius like Armstrong, jazz will continue to be created by a unique minority who are willing to sacrifice their lives for their art. It is a price no society has the right to demand of its artists.

The outlines of the story are known well enough. Armstrong grew up in New Orleans when jazz was in the ferment of creation, and by the time he was eighteen and joined King Oliver's jazz band in Chicago he was already one of the most brilliant instrumentalists in the new music. In the course of the next few years he made the trumpet the major jazz instrument (it was to remain so until Parker enforced the dominance of the saxophone from the 1940s onward), influenced not only all the trumpeters who followed him but pianists like Earl Hines and saxophonists like Coleman Hawkins as well, helped develop a new form of wordless singing (scat), and shaped the art of the jazz vocal—bringing it to a height which only a few great woman singers, such as Billie Holiday, have equalled.

More important, he exploded the classic forms of New Orleans/Chicago jazz, which throughout the 1920s was basically a music of group polyphony held together by strict improvisational canons. Through sheer personal creativity, Armstrong forced jazz into expressionism—much as Charlie Parker, once again, was later to wrench jazz into modernism. His Hot Seven solo on 'Wild Man Blues', for instance, is still the hottest and bluest solo recorded in jazz; a later performance, 'Tight Like This', is an expressionist masterpiece in which Armstrong builds from chorus to chorus to an inevitable and stunning climax. From there, it seemed, Louis Armstrong could go anywhere. He was the king, and everyone knew it.

What happened?

The Depression hit. The jazz bands broke up. The musicians were forced into obscurity, or died, or joined the commercial swing orchestras which purveyed romantic schmaltz to audiences unable to bear the grim reality around them. Armstrong formed just such an orchestra, turned himself into a consummate showman, and for twenty years survived by playing what the times and his fans demanded. Any jazz discography has page after page of the records Armstrong churned out during this period. With a few notable exceptions, they are worthless. As jazz critic Rudi Blesh, has written:'Although all of Louis Armstrong's work is impressive even in relation to all music, that from his mature period is in a field hostile to jazz and, it may be, to his own truest expression'.

Finally, after the Second War World, Armstrong returned to small group jazz and formed his All Stars. The world, however, had left him behind. A new generation of jazz revolutionaries—Monk, Parker, Christian, Powell—had refused to compromise, had overthrown the old order, and set jazz on a new course. And Armstrong was already an old man. We never heard the music he could have made.

We were left, instead, with Ambassador Satch. A few years

ago, when he was touring Australia with his All Stars, I heard Louis at Sydney Stadium. His concerts were the tired showbiz routines we (and no doubt he) had come to dread: not much jazz, schoolboy pyrotechnics and exhibitionism by each of the All Stars, with Armstrong spending most of his time on stage singing stale pop songs like 'Kiss To Build A Dream On' and 'Mack the Knife'. There were some superb moments, because he could still play great jazz when he wanted to, but he was an artist in a straitjacket—a prisoner of his audience and his own strict entertainment—first professionalism.

When he wasn't up front at the mike he sat on a special chair at the back of the revolving stage, his face in shadows, trumpet held on his knees, motionless. Sometimes he mouthed a word or two at one of his band. He looked old and drawn, and the one and a half hours he'd promised he'd be on stage must have seemed a long time. Occasionally he mopped his face with a handkerchief, or looked at the crowd with an expression which seemed to mix hostility and resignation. I found myself wondering what Armstrong, one of the great artists of our time, was thinking as he sat there in the darkness, his face only a few feet away from the spotlight focused on Trummy Young's vaudeville trombone act, the crowd screaming for an encore to an impossibly fast 'Tiger Rag'.

After the concert, when the audience had pushed its way out through the rainsoaked corridors of the stadium and the second-shift audience had begun to pour in, I went to see Louis where he was resting in his dressing-room. He was as gentle and considerate as ever, but tired, and when he spoke he scarcely bothered to move his lips. He was sitting, absolutely alone, in front of a dressing-table mirror. He had changed out of his sweat-soaked stage suit, and had a white apron tucked into his neck and spread across his chest. Another white kerchief was pinned across his forehead and back over his scalp. He had a special cream on his lips.

I asked him a few questions about jazz, and he answered slowly and almost absentmindedly. Did he play the same routine in every country? 'Yeah, we play it most every country—Tokyo, the States, we play the same thing everywhere.' Did he ever play straight jazz any more? 'Naw, we mix it up, you know—mix it up. That's the trouble with these jazz cats today. They play it drawn-out and monotonous, you know.' Did he ever play with musicians outside his own group? 'Naw.' Even at jazz festivals? 'We just play the same stuff.'

What about criticism by jazz writers of the way he stuck to an unvarying repertoire? 'You gotta play the tunes they ask for. That's what they want. You play something new and they ask you for the old songs.' Why didn't he play more and sing less? Louis paused before answering, looked down at the bare boards of the stadium floor. 'The folks like that stuff...'

When I left Louis had turned back to his mirror, sitting alone before it, utterly unmoving. Outside in the corridor Jewel Brown, his female vocalist, had her face in her hands; Trummy Young was pacing up and down. Beyond the door came the sound of hundreds of people jostling and pushing down towards the brilliantly lighted arena. I looked at the programme. With cruel poignancy it quoted an extract from *Time*: 'Oddly enough, Armstrong ... has been regarded in the United States less as an artist than a picturesque, Sambo-styled entertainer.'

And now he's dead.

I owe a lot to Louis Armstrong. He's been part of my life ever since, as a schoolboy of fourteen, I first heard of him. There are probably several million others like me throughout the world, for whom Armstrong has been a crucial part of their imagination and sensibility; and God knows how many more to whom he has given music, pleasure, and perhaps some insight into the greatness of jazz.

But it isn't enough. Until jazz is recognised for what it is, as one of the few profound art forms created in the last century, and is given the support which other 'high arts' receive as a matter of course, then jazzmen like Armstrong will have to struggle all their lives against an environment which is intrinsically hostile to them. And until it's also recognised that jazz is the classic music of black Americans (just as soul is their pop music), and that its lack of recognition is part of the racism American society practises against its black sub-culture, jazzmen will be confronted with a terrible choice between life and art. And the despairing story of Louis 'Pops' Armstrong, who was simply (and too early) the finest musician the revolutionary world of jazz has ever known, or is likely to know, will be repeated again and again and again.

1971

3. Blues Night in Harlem

Rain, black rain falling down 125th Street. Even the Apollo, lit up like a trans-Atlantic holiday liner, seems stranded in its garish pool of light. Though 125th Street is the main street in America's most sophisticated black community, there is hardly a building over four storeys and it looks like any other ghetto: rubbish everywhere, junked cars, boarded-up shopfronts, decay and disintegration—what was that again about institutionalised racism? We make it across the street to the ticket booth, up the precipitous flights of stairs to the balcony, and catch the tailend of the movie show. The feature is a cops-and-robbers, Z-grade; then Woody Woodpecker; then a badly dubbed black-and-white short of God knows how many years ago featuring, would you believe, Alan Arkin (he of the multi-million-dollars *Catch 22*) as a Puerto Rican dropout and made by (wait for it) the Maysles Brothers, lately of the Rolling Stones and *Gimme Shelter*. How the unknowns have grown. They needed to: by the time the movies flicker to a stop it is as tomblike inside the Apollo as it is turbulent outside and I think, man, *nothing* will ever be able to wake this audience from the dead.

I am wrong.

'Ladies and gentlemen, welcome to Blues Night at the Apollo.' People stir in their seats; comedian/MC Ed Gordon hobbles off the stage with a stiff leg. Everyone laughs. The huge curtain balloons, buffeted from outside, then sweeps aside to reveal bare boards, a background swathe of instruments and musicians, a chorus of four pink-satin-sheathed girl vocalists, a large black woman, a singer with a pencil moustache and an electric-blue suit, and a short guy in an open-necked shirt who is trying to shout above the background riff. Provincial repertory theatre, Maintown, U.S.A. It isn't until the guy in the open-necked shirt swings his guitar above his left shoulder and picks off a chorus of flawless single-string blues that I recognise B. B. King, introducing his show. He walks off, taking most of the others with him, and the satin-sheathed Robert Patterson Singers settle down to their first number.

It's OK, but it isn't until they settle down to a slow, preaching version of 'Abraham, Martin and John' that the responses start coming. 'Good God!' 'Sing it, sister.' 'Yeah!' They spread like random ripples around the theatre; people start sitting up and swaying; like, it is beginning to warm up. By the time the quartet had finished its last number with the lead singer strutting the stage like a sex gospeller, the Apollo crowd has thrown off Woody Woodpecker like a bad memory and is ready for action.

They get it. The hefty woman I saw before, looking much the way Bessie must have in her prime, comes onto the stage. She staggers a little: she is high, or loaded, or just overweight. The audience giggles, sympathetically. She grabs the mike, signals the band, and launches straight into a twelve-bar blues. It's fantastic: the power, the authority, sweeps out into that huge cavern of a showplace and gathers up the crowd in a single, warm, joyous clutch. Your heart lifts, people are clapping their hands, a high-voltage charge of energy leaps from fingertip to fingertip around the amphitheatre. When, after two choruses, she extracts a mouth harp from her voluminous pink robe and wails tight, beautifully phrased blues into the microphone, that Apollo audience—the toughest in American show business, they say—goes out of its mind. 'Hey!' 'Hey!' 'Good Gawd Almighty!' 'Play it!'

She stops, mumbles something about Janis Joplin, and blasts off into 'Ball and Chain'. Of course. It is Big Mama Thornton. And as she sings her way majestically through the song, ripping off high falsettos, breaks, swoops and shouts with the ease of a virtuoso artist, I realise just what Janis was after and never got near, what all that straining and posturing and little-girl-with-a-big-voice melodrama was about; it was about what

Big Mama Thornton, with apparently no effort and exquisite control, can achieve on any song at all.

Stop. 'Everyone's ripped off this song 'cept me,' says Big Mama bitterly. Then straight into 'Hound Dog'. Janis made her name by copying Big Mama's version of 'Ball and Chain'; Elvis did much the same with 'Hound Dog'. After just four beats, everyone, everyone, in the Apollo is clapping hands in time. The rhythm is momentous, irresistible, the offbeat as heavy as a ... ball and chain.

But then something starts to go wrong. The band takes a chorus, but it isn't together and by the time Big Mama starts singing again even she can't rescue it; the clapping fades. She moves imperceptibly into 'Walkin' the Dog', but the rhythm changes confusingly; the clapping stops altogether. Big Mama struts across the stage, walking her dog, and people laugh but they are not listening to the music any longer and, as she disappears into the wings, there is a burst of applause. But everyone is vaguely disappointed.

Why?

A soul singer in mini-skirt and outsize Afro follows. 'And now ladies and gentlemen, a change of pace, something in a different mood which I truly hope you'll enjoy ... ' The voice is cigarette-husky, the song a cliché and late-hour torch. After Big Mama, it is nothing.

Then comes Bobby Blue Bland, still in his blue suit. He has a soft, somewhat mannered voice and a throwaway stage style, but he sings the blues and nothing but the blues. By the second number his soft sexual message has begun to get through: 'Listen to that man,'says the woman in the red dress next to me. She and others are calling out quietly, answering the words of the songs. 'You can take me home any time, baby.' The mood builds up again. For a finale Bobby Bland does his hit number, 'Stormy Monday', and sings it impeccably—changing the dynamics, letting the volume wind down for a long middle section featuring a white cat on lead guitar, then working up to a still-relaxed climax. When he leaves the crowd is lively, joyous, expectant. B. B. King could harldy have wished for a better launching platform.

Comedian Ed Gordon reappears, raps for five minutes. Then the curtains billow, draw back. 'Ladies and gentlemen, *The*

King!' And sure enough it is: B. B. in dark evening suit, his band drawn up behind him, his guitar Lucille flashing and glittering in the spotlights and that throaty voice shouting: 'All I need is a little bit of love ...' It's his warm-up, interspersed with a bit of showbiz patter, and then straight into an uptempo version of 'Why I Sing the Blues'. It's so good, so strange/familiar that Blues Night at the Apollo seems about to come to its appropriate climax.

It doesn't. B. B. chops the song short after two choruses (okay, so maybe he's tired of it), draws up a chair, and launches off into a long monologue in which he describes his own career— but talking about himself in the third person. 'Sometimes he got booed, and there was pain in his heart, so much pain that at night he cried, alone ...' It is smooth, professional, a carefully worked out showbiz routine, broken up by single-line snatches of blues; but it is also embarrassing, and very self-indulgent, and by the time B. B. is halfway through the audience is tired of it. Rightly. 'Sing it, man.' 'Don't give us that shit, man, play it.'

B. B. perseveres, and against a rising barrage of interjections reaches his peroration: 'And now here he is before you, B. B. King!' The band breaks out into an uptempo blues, and everyone's spirits rise again. He is The King, ain't no doubt about it; one of the outstanding blues singers and guitarists of our time, at the height of his power, self-confident and in control. But then B. B. chops the music again and launches into another showbiz routine; a long, imaginary conversation between a faithless man and a faithless woman. The shouts start up again; they came here to hear blues, man. A woman down the front interrupts one of B. B.'s more extravagant flights of rhetoric with a quip that brings the house down; B. B. can't go on, loses his cool, turns back to his band and tries a slow blues, one of his recent hits: 'Chains and Things'. It starts off okay, then falls apart: the band is uneasy, out of balance, the piano sounds like a man hitting an empty gasoline tin with a stick, and even though B. B. tries his best he can't rescue it. Even 'The Thrill Is Gone' doesn't work. A final fast blues—but by now it is really hopeless and even a flashy guitar solo by B. B. can't disguise that fact. Nobody is clapping, and when the end comes the audience greets it with a mixture of relief and disappointment: so that was The King?

Outside it is still raining, and two hustlers are flogging glossy pin-ups of B. B. and Bobby Bland. Hardly anyone buys. In the gutters outside the Apollo, the rubbish is still there, rainproof, indestructible.

What went wrong?

A week later I am still trying to figure it out. One thing is for sure: B. B. misjudged his audience. As Mama Thornton and Bobby Bland showed, they were ready for hard, gutsy blues—the rill thing, as little Richard might say. Instead B. B. played down to them, resorted to showbiz tricks. I've seen Louis Armstrong do the same. It's as though neither of them trusted the music itself any longer, and had been forced to turn themselves into actors.

B. B. King, it seems to me, is in trouble. His recent albums have shown a decline from *Live and Well*, the record which blasted him into the charts, the Fillmore East and a large audience of white listeners. *Indianola Mississippi Seeds* is marred by lush, over-insistent strings. The band he had at the Apollo couldn't even handle the rhythms of some of his hit discs. And now, in what is the most bitter irony of all, B. B. seems to be misjudging his own audience; he plays undiluted blues for white kids in downtown Manhattan, and feeds his own people showbiz corn.

But there is more to it than that. It is a truism that racism is so built into the American entertainment industry—and the society for which showbiz is a vulgarly bejewelled magnifying glass—that it is the white artists who rip off black music, the white artists who get the gold records while the originators are left behind on the one-night-gig circuit which stretches from Chicago to Oakland. What I didn't understand until the Apollo, however, was the extent to which racism isn't just a barrier but a cruelly destructive acid which disfigures and distorts the back artists who are its victims. It makes them distrust their own music, forces them to conform to acceptable stereotypes, stunts their capacity for growth. By depriving them of the success they need and deserve, it deprives them of the freedom which any artist needs to develop, think, mature.

Take Big Mama Thornton. If she had anything like the

opportunities or skilful management which inferior white artists get, she would never make the obvious mistakes she committed the other night. She would have a band of her own, for a start. And there would be half a dozen shrewd heads watching her performance, analysing and criticising it, polishing it, making sure that the fervour she arouses with a song like 'Hound Dog' isn't dissipated, but has some chance for release— which means making it clear when the song has ended and giving the audience some chance to participate, if only by applause. A Mick Jagger or a Janis Joplin would have made sure of that. Big Mama hardly has a chance.

It's a vicious circle, because until she achieves the expertise she needs she probably won't make that crucial breakthrough and will remain just another black singer whose music is ripped off by white imitators who have the necessary money and time and (to be fair) the taste to realise that the music they borrow is better than their own.

Of course, there are dangers in over-emphasising the stage performance bit. You can end up, as so many rock stars do, by substituting hype for music: remember Jim Morrison? But a rock or blues or soul concert is as much a theatrical experience as a musical one, and theatre has always been concerned with the deliberate projection of images. In his own muddled way B. B. King is grappling with this problem in his stage routine; it's scarcely his fault that he is uncertain just who his audience is, or why they are there, or what they want him to do. Which is symbolic: even black artists who *do* make the breakthrough pay unsuspected penalties. What's happened to Sly? Why did Aretha crack up in full flight? Jimi Hendrix?

I don't know. Rain falling across Harlem; forlorn Christmas lights strung across 125th Street like intersecting crucifixes; car lamps like giant searchlights. Something cripples a Big Mama Thornton; keeps Bobby Bland, a gifted though not great artist, from achieving anything like his full potential; distorts even a fine blues performer like B. B. King. After the concert, a sense of immense promise unfulfilled, of cheating, of a tragic flaw in the heartfelt centre of it all. *Ladies and Gentlemen, Blues Night.* Wipe yer hand across yer mouth and laugh. Question: does the Apollo exist? Answer: no. In a metaphysical sense black America, even the Apollo, is really a projection of white America's hostility, fantasies and fearful imagination.

Or was.

Rerun. Walking down that long Apollo lobby, I am surrounded by Afros, dashikis, gaudy black gear. Everyone is talking, super-alive, gesturing with arms and tote bags, a suppressed power crackling amid the laughter and half-shouts. There are a few white students around, bearded, harbingers of the hopeful new togetherness, but they look lost and a little apprehensive. I get swept along by the crowd, jostled, feeling like an extra in *Les Enfants du Paradis*, as it pours in an irresistible torrent of humanity out the swing doors. It is still raining. The rubbish is still there in the gutter. But I don't think they'll stand much longer for that shit.

1972

America in the 1970s

4. Soundtrack for a Bad Movie

Of course, you can't tell a country by its music. So they say.

Early summer. WABC New York is pumping out bland city rock. It gets so you can't tell the hits from the Coke ads: in a commercial society everything (eventually) gets commercialised. So we pile the kids, four of them, into the Volkswagen camper and make off. To find America's music. And America . . .

We head south. It's a surprise to find it starts at Washington: cracker accents, grey marble, a blind man and his dog begging on the corner. White Capitol, black ghettos. On the AM radio, white schmaltz, black soul. It is a motif which is to be repeated.

Virginia. In high wooded country which runs up into the Appalachians we find a camp ground called Beaver Run: frogs, dragonflies and beavers a mile down the wilderness trail. The manager, John Hills, is a telegraph linesman; he notices my guitar outside the tent and that night turns up with his own, an acoustic Gibson. We sit with the children around the smoky fire and he begins playing in a flat-pick style which strokes across all six strings, creating a rich chordal sound. His first few songs are country and western hits, but then he starts singing white gospel songs in a full baritone which lends itself to easy harmonising; his wife, a shy girl from west Virginia, joins in with a high, clear voice and for a moment it could almost be the Carter family singing one of those spirituals which date from the great religious revival of the nineteenth century.

It turns out that John and his brother play each Sunday in

their local church, using two electric guitars and two powerful Fender amplifiers to keep pace with the congregation (even the churches have turned electric). It is a revivalist sect, where they sing loud and hold onto their notes. Yeah, says John, he likes singing. Everyone around here likes singing. Church is where they do most of it.

I remember what a friend of mine once said about white spirituals: simple music for a simple people. Well, no people are simple. But the music is: easy melodies, straightforward harmonies. Like the religion, it is fundamentalist. The roads around here wind across timbered slopes to neat, well-kept towns grouped around neat, well-attended churches. They are at peace. Middle America: the great heartland, home of the brave, muscle cars, and Nixon's constituency. When I play some traditional ballads for John, picking out the melody of those lonesome love songs on the treble strings, he looks puzzled and describes them as 'folky'. For that real mountain music, he says, we will have to go to the Appalachians.

A day later we are there. We drive through Crozet, belting out country and western sounds from its tiny foothills radio station, and then strike the hollows which run up into the Appalachians. I begin to realise why the push to the west was halted here for a century, creating a rich folk culture of myths and music which later spilled out onto the plains: the mountains are dense, dark, impenetrable. Moonshine and puritanism. And poverty. Each dead-end road reproduces stark black-and-white snapshots from the 1930s: deserted, rotting two-storey houses crumbling sideways into thorn bushes; thin, lonely roads which wind through dense forest, open out into a cluster of shacks and trailer homes, then close over again; creeks which disappear into bracken gloom; an old store at an unmarked crossroad and nothing, absolutely nothing, for miles around. It is getting dark; I am lost in a maze of unfamiliar valleys: Brown's Cove, Sugar Hollow, Bacon Hollow. Trying to turn around on a narrow road which has petered out into yet another dead end, I back the Volkswagen into a ditch and have to be pushed out by local farmers who have been watching quizzically. Shiflett Hollow? Yup, about three mile further north, but you have to backtrack another ten or fifteen.

At last I find one of the families which still play the old mountain music. The head of the family picks banjo. ('His wife give him a banjo for his birthday, she couldn't stand that fiddle no longer.') He lives in a trailer home with chickens scratching in the dirt outside the front door, grubby Depression children playing among the old tyres and junked and rusty autos. He has had to go and help his neighbour on the next door farm cut some hay and at ten o'clock on that brilliant, moonlit night they are still working. His wife, barefooted, curses the kids as they fight and squall. Somewhere up in a high clearing a fox is barking.

The grandmother, a shrewd, wizened woman about five feet tall, appears from a gloomy, two-storey Tobacco Road house hidden by trees and the decaying undergrowth which used to be the front garden. She lives there alone. Don't know why the gov'nmint don't do more for poor people. No work around here: no land worth farming neither. No, ain't many niggers around here, though there are one or two of 'em at the local school. She got nothin' agin 'em, but you know what young 'uns are like: you wouldn't like your daughter havin' a kid by one of 'em, would ya? Poor whites: the only thing they have left to be proud of is their skin. And their music.

The banjo picker's brother wanders over. He has a guitar and plays it in a deft, flat-pick style which reminds me of Jack Elliott, one-time travelling mate of Woody Guthrie. It's good, but it's not what I've come to hear. It's after midnight before the banjo player gets back from his neighbour's farm. He has nicotined teeth, several missing, a thin undernourished frame, sloping shoulders: the physique of poverty the world over. But his music is superb: he plays banjo in pre-Scruggs style, a jagged ragtimey music which stretches right back to the early pioneer settlements, square dances, hoedowns and chest-level fiddlers. The flat, plangent notes flick out into the night. In that high mountain country the traditional folk melodies and simple banjo arpeggios seem inevitable; you play them because only single, unadorned notes seem fitting in that crisp and starblack air. Anthropomorphism? Perhaps.

Early in the morning, driving back to where I have pitched the tent, the hollows and ridges of the Appalachians pass as in a dream, a tranced series of static motifs, glazed in moonlight.

Has a century, two centuries, really gone by?

We spend a week in the Appalachians. In the Blue Ridge Mountains, not far from where the Carter family lived, local people are still making beautiful handcrafted dulcimers ... and a quill to play with. In the Great Smokies we camp next to a family from Jean Ritchie country, in Kentucky. Over breakfast their seven-year-old daughter, Toni, sings a mountain version of the old ballad 'Pretty Milking Maid' which I've never heard before; she's 'skeered', but finally lets me record her on tape. We turn west, climb in dense fog across the highest pass in the eastern chain, headlamps turned an eerie yellow; thunderstorm; then down, circling like a marsh bird, towards Tennessee. Behind us the Smokies are lost in cloud.

Nashville. A dingy, provincial town which reflects exactly the hard, barren, God-fearing country we have been driving through: at every intersection in east Tennessee, a billboard for Christ. In Tootsie's Orchid Lounge, hangout of every country and western songwriter with a crumpled lyric in his hip pocket, I run into Kris Kristofferson, one of the new generation of Nashville cats who have wrenched country and western out of its old, stale conventions and revitalised it with folk and pop idioms: he has written the music for Dennis Hopper's *The Last Movie* and his song 'Me and Bobby McGee' was Janis Joplin's last hit.

At Monument Records, Kris listens to the final studio mix of his 'Sunday Morning, Coming Down', a single from his own album and a hit for Johnny Cash as well. Another bar, and then Kris and I go backstage at the Grand Ole Opry to take in the show.

There have been lines outside most of the day, and that huge barn of a showplace is packed. There are some top musicians on the bill, including banjo player Earl Scruggs, originator of the virtuoso Scruggs style of banjo picking, and guitarist Lester Flatt, each with his own group since they broke up. But the music is appalling: slick, conventional, unfelt. The only performance in which any of the original emotional impulse remains, that plaintive cry of the heart which still lingers on in the Appalachians, is a white blues performed by Scruggs and his mouth-harp player; but it receives exactly the same reception, no better and no worse, from that happy redneck audience as all the Hank Williams imitators on stage in their Stetsons, cowboy suits and spangled harmonies. I have the feeling that I am watching the last, empty rites of a once meaningful ritual: the forms are still there, the nasal voices and twanging guitars and gospel harmonies, but the heart has been hollowed out of the music and only the shell remains.

Kris splits. On the AM radio, Tony Joe White, another of the Nashville new wave: a mod fusion of country, blues and rock. Perhaps the function of country music now is to infuse rock with that transcendental white spiritualism that was distilled, along with moonshine whisky, in the smoky heights of Appalachia, that went west with Jimmie Rodgers and Hank Williams, and has now begun to permeate country rock: thus The Band; Crosby, Stills, Nash & Young; James Taylor. The new whiteface minstrels.

Outside Nashville, Interstate 65. At the far end, nearly a thousand miles further south: New Orleans.

Ever since I was a kid at school, I've been listening to jazz. I began with Louis Armstrong, Jelly Roll Morton, the blues of Bessie Smith, and then discovered the jazz of the New Orleans revival: Bunk Johnson, George Lewis, Kid Ory, Jim Robinson, Kid Howard. My first instrument was a clarinet, on which I tried to imitate George Lewis's beautiful 'Burgundy Street Blues'; even when I'd worked my way forward to Charlie Parker, John Coltrane and Albert Ayler, I never stopped listening to the music from which it all sprang. New Orleans occupies a large place in my head.

But the Crescent City is still a surprise: barely American, more like Marseilles in the New World. Wharves, seafront boulevards, gumbo, red beans and rice, Dixie beer, showplace paddle boats, the Mississippi in brown half-flood. And then the names: Shreveport, which I learnt from Jelly Roll's 'Shreveport Stomp', Lake Pontchartrain, Burgundy Street, Canal Street, Rampart, Perdido—even Basin Street! The streets are crowded with tramcars, but American hustle has slowed to a more casual, more European pace. There is a fantastic mixture of people—black, white, French, Spanish, Chinese, Italian, quarter-caste, half-caste, Creole—and they seem to get on more easily together than in most other places in America (though I see a solitary Black Panther who spies the VW, grins, joyfully sells me a copy of the party's paper). Half a century ago it was one of the world's great seaports, and it is a spectacularly hybrid city still (New Orleans, not New York, was the great melting pot); and it was no accident that jazz, a hybrid if ever there was one, began there and nowhere else. White marching bands, black blues and folk music. French classicism, Creole artistry . . .

Early that evening I follow Bourbon Street from the city centre down to the Vieux Carré, the French quarter. The transformation from the cool drowsiness of the day is startling: open doors, bars every three or four shopfronts, blazing lights, crowds spilling from the sidewalks into the narrow streets, and everywhere music. So much music! Jazz is dead in New Orleans, people had told me. They're crazy. There is jazz at almost every intersection, jazz swirling out of the open bar windows, jazz drifting up from basement clubs, jazz blasting out of juke boxes and dance halls, usually smoother and more professional than on those scratchy 78 r.p.m. discs I have at home but still the old, joyous sound. At one street-corner bar, Thomas Jefferson, a gifted black trumpeter, is leading a trad group with a Scandinavian clarinettist sitting in. Further up Bourbon Street, a five-piece group of younger New Orleans musicians is playing to an audience of hippies, tourists, locals. Blues pianist Roosevelt Sykes is at the Nero: I drop in, catch the last number of his set.

Then I turn towards the wharves and Preservation Hall. It is jammed up against other buildings and to get in you have to walk through a darkened side-entrance. As I enter, a tall, stooped black musician holding a trombone emerges from the gloom; it is Jim Robinson, one of the great New Orleans jazzmen, slide horn for Bunk and George Lewis, and someone I have been listening to on records and admired for twenty years. He walks onto the low dais, which is set in front of rows of benches, and the band slowly assembles: DeDe Pierce on cornet, his wife Billie at the upright piano, Willie Humphrey on clarinet, Marvin Kimball on banjo, Chester Zardiz on slap bass, Cie Frazier on drums. They are old men, most of them, members of that incredible first wave which created a profoundly original art form; it is remarkable that one man, like DeDe or Louis Armstrong, can span in his lifetime the entire history of jazz.

DeDe stomps his foot four times and off they go. The music is light, informal, and at first the cornet lead is so reticent that the jazz seems to lack a centre: is this what collective improvisation was all about, a group sound in which no one dominated? Billie Pierce brings the blues back with a high, piercing vocal on 'Pallet on the Floor', the theme song of Storyville's prostitutes when it was the red light centre of America. By now DeDe has begun to warm up and the next number, 'Honky Tonk Rag', is almost flawless: long, repeated glissandi from Jim Robinson which slide upwards with DeDe's cornet response dancing along the top of the notes, the clarinet dark and willowy, the rhythm section loosely together . . . it is so beautifully phrased and interknit, so complete, that I understand exactly what classicism means and why this is known, rightly, as classic jazz. No wonder it took over the world.

The rag ends, and Willie Humphrey beckons someone who is standing in the darkened hallway at my back. 'Hey, come'n sit in.' Whoever it is won't be persuaded. The band plays a last number, breaks up. I talk briefly with Jim Robinson; he is over seventy now, but hardly looks it. Willie Humphrey walks over to the friend he invited to sit in. He is a short, compact guy in a suit and open-necked shirt; drifting past, I have just time to recognise Dizzy Gillespie, who is playing a gig at Al Hirt's on Bourbon Street.

Roots, man.

Deeper roots. It is a hot Sunday, and we are driving north along Highway 61, heading for Natchez. For two days we have been following the Mississippi as it curls and loops through Louisiana, the river invisible for most of the time because of the grassy levee banks which guard it; they look so peaceful, grazed by a few stray cows, that it's easy to forget the human agony which built them: black chain gangs, black slaves, black mule teams.

Good mornin', Capt'n, good mornin', son,
Good mornin', Capt'n, good mornin', son,
Do you need another mule skinner on your new mule run?

Every now and then, set well back from the leaves, we pass imperial white-columned plantation houses standing like miniature Parthenons amid barbered lawns and landscaped weeping willows, and in between are the pitiful, straggling villages which, with their tumbledown shacks set on stilts and black people in armchairs on decrepit porches and creeper-clad trees that shut out the sun, have been carved by brute force out of the Louisiana bayous and seem not to have changed since slavery. Of course, the people are free now.

On the right we pass a small clearing with yards and high fences and automobiles parked helter-skelter behind the slip-rails. A rodeo is going on. I drive on, because we are behind schedule and the south has filled me with unease: there is a pervasive feeling of institutionalised violence, of a society terribly becalmed. Faulkner, Oxford, Jackson. But the children are thirsty, and we have been on the road for a couple of hours without a break. I turn the camper around and drive up to the gate. An immensely fat guy with a narrow-brimmed hat and cigar looks at us, hesitates, then extracts a dollar before waving us inside the compound. The kids tumble out onto the dusty sun-caked ground, and we assemble in an untidy knot: a man with a beard, a woman with hippie-length red hair and four blonde kids under six.

We are the only white people there. The rest, maybe a hundred, are black: black cowboys in chaps and spurs and Stetsons, black farmhands in Levis and red shirts, black women in cheap cotton dresses and spectacles, black children with bare feet and dusty legs and inquiring faces. There are horses in the corrals, saddle horses tied up to the high rodeo railings, a few calves in the main arena which cowboys canter after in a desultory fashion, swinging lariats. We walk over to the railings and the children peer through the slats at the horses. Nobody stares at us, but everyone is very aware of us. They are not hostile, but we feel unwanted. The heat stokes up towards a Mississippi midday. Nobody talks to us. The children feel it and keep close—all except the two-year-old, who keeps running off. Knots of children swirl by. Should we stay?

It's solved, sort of, by a youngish black cowboy who nonchalantly walks his horse across to us and asks us where we're from. New York. Yeah, he thought so; he can pick the accent. (In fact it's Australian.) He tries to put us at ease, jokes with the kids, then asks if I have any grass. He doesn't believe me when I say no. C'mon, man, you from New York? And no grass? Even a little? No. But he is still full of love, peace and happiness. Man, he's worked in the city, he gets stoned whenever he can: grass, hash, acid. Sure, you can git acid even 'round here.

Our eldest daughter, Kate, reaches out towards his horse; would she like a ride? By this time I've had a good look at his pupils: he is stoned out of his mind, can't sit the horse properly, his reflexes slow and leaden. But before I can stop her, my wife hoists Kate up onto the railings and passes her over to the cowboy. He wheels and walks her around the dusty rodeo arena, then back. I wasn't afraid he'd let her come to any harm, was I? he mumbles. No, man.

Behind us, where the cars are parked, three guys are bent inside the raised hood of a pickup truck. They are big tough-looking men in gaudy shirts, and they don't seem to belong here: townies, maybe from Natchez. One of them beckons to me. I walk over slowly. He points to the knife I have sheathed in my belt. It's a Norwegian hunting knife, lent to me by a southerner who is my neighbour in New York—and a veteran of the civil rights marches. Don't take a gun where you're going, he told me; it can only get you into trouble. But take this knife. During the trip I have learnt to handle it, work it, throw it. Now they want it: from the way they are watching me I can tell it is to some extent a put-on, a deliberate challenge. I walk back to the camper, unlock it and give them a short-bladed kitchen knife. They start hacking at wires trailing from the distributor.

Midday. More people arriving, some of them in pickups lugging horse trailers. Unexpectedly, I hear a trombone at my back. Over near the shack, beneath the shade of a grotesquely stunted tree, a nuggety man in his sixties is shaking spittle out of his slide. Beside him is a younger man setting up drums, and another is plugging his electric guitar into a portable amplifier. It's the local band, come to play for the rodeo.

After half an hour, a few beers and a lot of clowning, they're ready to go. A long slide from the trombone man, and they blast off into an uptempo blues: the trombone takes the lead, playing short, staccato phrases in marching band style, with the guitar playing rhythmic boogie woogie runs and the drums rattling along behind. It's real southern juke music, a good-timey blend of blues and jazz: raucous, gutbucket, with a infectious brazen quality which rings out over that dusty rodeo ground and brings children a-running. After a while some of the men and women gather round too, leaning back on wooden benches dragged into the shade and beating time with their feet.

A break, and I go and get my tape recorder. The drummer, who is the leader, grins and gets me to set the microphone up next to his own portable mike. He is Hezekiah Early from Natchez; works as a mechanic by day, does the occasional gig at night and weekends. His guitarist is Jesse Wear, who can pick out blues leads but prefers to play Bo Diddley-like bass runs to keep the rhythm going. And the trombone man is L. P. (Pee Wee) Whittaker, a friendly, lighthearted old man who has played in more jazz bands than he cares to remember; hell, man, he's been playing all his life. He's popular with the crowd, most of whom seem to know him: 'Oh, you really gittin' goin' on that thang, Pee Wee,' shouts one of them. A few teenage girls start dancing, the men clapping hands and cheering them on; everyone starts to relax, smiles, becomes friendly and talkative. I realise how uptight I've been.

For the next two hours I tape everything the band does, playing the tape back after each number. Hezekiah is pleased with the sound. He's the vocalist, with a dark cutting voice which reminds me of early Memphis Slim, but sometimes one of the cowboys grabs the mike and sings archaic, half-chanted blues which sound like those early work songs recorded in the south by the Lomaxes for the Library of Congress. One jump backwards: Africa. One jump forward: rhythm and blues, rock, the pop music of the Western world. This is where it began, and this is where it's still going on. 'Heritage music', the avant-garde jazz pianist Danny Mixon calls it. He was talking about the black heritage, but now the world shares it. The black slave's gift to his white slave master . . . a revolution.

The three men from the battered pickup walk across and, without a word, hand my knife back. I stick it in a wooden railing, forget about it; it's still there. The cowboy who befriended us in the first place goes up to my wife.

'You want to be careful 'bout doin' things like this.'

'Don't you think we should be here?'

'There's some real mean white people in Natchez. They see you here, you could be in real bad trouble.'

Natchez. The old cotton capital, lynchpin of the south's slave system. And, later, of the lynch system. Howlin' Wolf, the Chicago rhythm and blues man, sings a blues about it: 'Natchez Burnin'. We leave the rodeo before dusk, hurrying to reach the Natchez Traceway and the national park before it gets too dark. An hour later, at a lonely intersection in that tangled Mississippi forest, a mid-1960s automobile loaded with white youths pulls up to our left. We have halted at the stop sign. They stare at our overburdened Volkswagen, weighed down with 12 x 12 tent, camping gear, child's stroller. One of them aims an imaginary rifle and pumps six bullets at us: one for me, one for my wife, one for each child. I turn right and drive off through the hastening gloom towards Natchez Traceway. The car doesn't follow.

It is midnight before the tent is up, everyone fed, the children asleep. We are the only people in the park, probably for miles and miles around; the campfire throws shifting, uncertain shadows against those enormous Mississippi tree trunks. I listen to the tapes of the black juke band, that strange mixture of sorrow, despair and excitement which created the blues, and to the bizarre night noises which, unidentified, zero in towards the flames. For the first time since we set out across America I begin to think I should have brought a rifle.

Houston. Country rock mishmash in a cellar clip joint, clipped black soul in an upstairs joint which demands two I.D.s per person. I try to track down blues singer Lightnin' Hopkins, who lives in Houston, but nobody seems to know where he is. Maybe, says someone, he's at one of the local rodeos . . .

Mexico. Spanish guitarists in the main plaza of Saltillo, flamenco strums and bossa nova rhythms. In the two-storey arcade which is the town market, a blind old man is propped against the stairs strumming a primitive, homemade harp.

Albuquerque. Chicano bar, Chicano bouncers in Nazi-style uniforms, Chicano rock group straight out of the 1950s: honking rock n' roll sax from a balding, middle-aged lush, out-of-time rhythm section, lead guitarist with lank black hair and a savagely beautiful, aquiline Indian face. His solo: Chuck Berry's 'Johnny B. Goode'. The dance floor is straight out of the 1950s too: most of the people are middle-aged, lipsticked and rouged, dancing waltz steps or grotesque parodies of the twist. The guards bounce a drunken white guy in open-necked shirt and suit for pestering women to dance with him, check the I.D. of anyone who looks under thirty. Along the bar, a row of grizzled mahogany faces staring at the dance floor or hunched over cans of Budweiser. These are the marginal people, the ghosts: Indians, Chicanos, strung like slaughtered chickens between two cultures, degraded by racism and total loss of identity. The substitutes: beer and violence. The guards carry guns.

The vibes are bad. I leave—Albuquerque, New Mexico, the south—and head for the west coast. It's got to be better.

It is. We reach Berkeley: psychedelic taxis, street people in Telegraph Avenue, cool sun on white concrete, force-fed pot plants in neon-lit clothes closets. On the campus, hip students throng around two folk guitarists doing their thing on the edge of Sproul Plaza, singing in high nasal voices. Along University Avenue, a guy with shoulder-length hair is sitting cross-legged over a mountain dulcimer, dispensing with the drones and plucking the melody out with his fingers, string by string, in a way I've never seen before: it sounds beautiful, as lyrical as anything I heard in the Appalachians. At B.B.B. department store on San Pablo the camera salesman plays blues guitar in the style of Mississippi John Hurt; the sporting goods guy is a tall black singer who is rehearsing his own vocal group.

There's music everywhere. Bronze Hog and Sky at New Orleans House; John Lee Hooker at the Matrix; a fine soul group, the Windy City Five, at the Lucky 13; Ike and Tina Turner and jazz-organ combos in Oakland, Bobby Bland in San Francisco. The AM radio plays better soul music than I've ever heard on the east coast; the apple wine ads leave Harlem chart-toppers for dead. Even the juke boxes are heavy. In a tiny hamburger joint in Oakland, a juke box with ten B. B. King singles.

The hamburger joint is opposite the church where Huey Newton gave Jonathon Jackson a Black Panther 'revolutionary funeral'. Jackson died in the Marin County shoot-up. Jackson's brother George was one of the Soledad prisoners. He's dead too. Every day the police, in khaki uniforms and guns, sweep along Telegraph Avenue and arrest kids who have come to Berkeley for the summer; anyone who is under eighteen is arrested on the spot, thrown into prison, sent home. Reagan calls it 'cleaning up Berkeley'. The people retaliate: one night a black guy in an Afro walks up to San Francisco's only Japanese-descent policeman, who is rebuking a student for making a U-turn in University Avenue. He talks quietly to the cop about Vietnam, pulls out a gun, shoots the cop's head off. The local underground papers, the *Tribe* and the *Barb*, preach revolution; the bank and shop windows along Telegraph are still boarded up from the last trashing. Reagan turns the board of regents loose on U.C.L.A. . . .

It doesn't take long to realise that the west coast is fantastically polarised, a breeding ground for extremes: Reagan, Haight-Ashbury, Chavez, Cleaver, Nixon, Lockheed, Hollywood, Watts, the immensely powerful men who control southern California's industry and finance, Hell's Angels, beavers, Sutter Cinema porno and a black community which is harried and victimised by some of the most vicious police in America. It is no accident that the John Birchers and the Black Panthers both began in California. The place is very, very uptight . . .

It all ends one night when I go to hear Ornette Coleman at Mandrake's, a club in Berkeley. It is packed, mainly with black guys and black women and a few white students. Afros dashikis, turbans, lion-tooth necklaces: the outward symbols of an inward awakening. Ornette is one of the key figures in the avant-garde jazz movement, a major innovator, and he is playing the music of the black revolution: anguished, free-form, apparently chaotic, the timbres harsh and insistent and unforgiving. The avant-garde has returned to the New Orleans concept of a communal music, a music of the people, but they have redefined it in terms of a freedom which is both musical and political. Each musician plays what he chooses: often there is no regular rhythm, no fixed melodic structure, hardly any solos, simply a breathtaking and agonising barrage of sound.

Ornette starts on trumpet, but as the set builds up in intensity he switches to soprano sax. He rips off long virtuoso runs and phrases which bring gasps at the sheer daring of it, the bass, drums and tenor sax creating a tidal momentum over which the soprano soars and whorls in whiplash arabesques. People are swaying trance-like in their seats, a guy four rows from the front is bent over double swinging his head, there is a strange dichotomy between those who are shaking uncontrollably to the music and those who are sitting motionless, very stoned, but all are utterly involved in what Ornette Coleman and the group are doing.

It is the last set, and when it is over an explosion of held breath rises from the crowd like incense. We have been celebrants in a holy ceremony. People smile, shake their heads, arising from hypnosis.

The bar closes. Outside it is a warm summer night, people standing around on the sidewalk. Such a good scene, man; why destroy it by walking away? I lean up against a lamp post and dig the talk and one guy who is dancing little steps up and down the pavement one two three one two up and down and around in tiny circles and playing a little cane flute with a range of about five notes but he is playing his heart out and it sounds good while the others in dashikis and Coleman-type hats laugh and move around and then Ornette appears and answers questions from one of them, stooped over and serious with sax case tucked under one arm, before he splits and so very slowly the scene disintegrates and I decide it is time to go home. I climb into the camper, grimy with dust from Mexico and half the United States, and drive along San Pablo and then left up Blake Street through the black section of Berkeley towards the campus and switch the radio onto the local soul station and because the jazz has been so moving, so exhilarating, I turn it way up loud and so set off home along Blake Street, Berkeley in the United States with a sort of fierce exultation in my blood and Aretha Franklin in my ears

And so I do not hear the siren

The first thing I notice is the red light in my rear vision mirror, the red light on top of the prowl car twitching and twirling

So I ease my way very slowly and very carefully across the next intersection and pull over to the kerb in this quiet suburban street, the houses in darkness and streetlights masked by trees, and turn the radio off

And wait

Because by now the prowl car has pulled up behind me, the siren still screaming and the light flashing round and round, and as two cops jump out another police car accelerates up the street and jams itself in front of the camper in case I try to escape and the doors swing open and police hit the ground before it has even stopped

Two cops, one white and one black, appear at my window and order me into the street so I get down out of the camper and the first thing I notice is that the white cop is very nervous and jumpy, he is pale and talking very fast and the first thing he says is are you armed and I say no but immediately he runs his hands down my body past my knees then straightens up with the other cops moving up in the background and then says are you on drugs and I say no but very quickly he whips out a flashlight and grabbing my jaw thrusts it left, right, while he shines the flashlight into my pupils, right, left

It has all happened so fast, it has happened much faster than I can describe it, that I am trying to get myself together when another police car with siren howling comes fast down Blake Street and broadsides to a halt on the other side of the road opposite me so that now I am surrounded by three squad cars and the police jump out but this time I notice they are carrying shotguns and one of them takes up position against the rear fender of the police car with shotgun at the ready and another stands down near the front and a third walks across the narrow grass verge to an absolutely blank wall and turns around and stands guard with the shotgun held Mexican-wise across his body, every action so deliberate and well-drilled and practised that I think Christ! I have seen this somewhere before in a bad movie

But I wasn't in it

Meanwhile the cop is cross-questioning me: name age identity (which for once I do not have on me) so he says where you from and I say New York and it turns out this is bad because they simply gaol 'itinerants' who do not have I.D.s so then he asks me have I been drinking but before I reply he forces my head down to smell my breath with the radio transmitter in the squad car behind me rattling off messages and descriptions and the shotgun men on the other side of the road standing immobile except for the guy against the wall who has got down on one knee for Chrissake with the shotgun pointed forward and just a little above my head and looking at the faces of these cops in the pale lamplight I realise that I only have to make one stupid move, one false move like reaching inside the camper for proof of I.D., and these cops who are very uptight will just shoot my bloody head off

So then I begin to think quite understandably that they have made a mistake, that they are after someone else who looks like me or a camper that looks like mine, so I say so to the cop and he says no, they aren't after anyone, I was doing 35 m.p.h. in a 25 m.p.h. zone and I didn't stop as soon as the siren went off so he sent out a chase alarm because 'we try to cover each other'

And at first they are going to gaol me on the spot but talking very quietly and not moving I finally convince them that I am who I say I am and the scales tilt one way and then the other and then the white cop gets on the transmitter to H.Q. to find out what to do and at last comes back and says no he won't imprison me after all he will just book me because you understand I was doing 35 m.p.h. oh sure of course that's pretty bad

With the cops with their shotguns still there watching leaning back against the squad car and kneeling beside the wall

So he books me and slowly everything cools down enough for me to get back into the V.W. and drive up Blake Street towards my home which is just five blocks away

And this time I don't turn the radio on.

And I think, if the cops act like this over me, how do they act if you are black? or a hippie? or a Panther? or Ornette Coleman? or one of any other of the outcast groups which make up the mass of America?

Knowing the answer already, because in the end it is the society, the culture, which creates the music and it is no accident that in the ghetto the music is the music of revolution just as Watts Newark Detroit were no accidents either and though the incident has already turned surreal, a nightmare in another country, it reveals a surreal truth: Natchez New Orleans Oakland Nashville Appalachia—each has created music out of deprivation, the music of America is the music of slaves ex-slaves poor whites hillbillies farmhands illiterates immigrants revolutionaries minorities people who have poured into their art everything which they have never been free to enact in their lives and so have created for oppressed, alienated twentieth-century humanity a music which, appropriately enough, has at its black/white/yellow heart a type of cry.

The next day I pick up a couple of hitch-hikers, a quiet young couple who have been living in a rural commune in Oregon and who have come to Berkeley to shop at the co-op, and because I have decided to leave the west coast I tell them about what happened the night before and I say, it was like something out of a bad movie.

And he says, America is a bad movie.

1971

5. Up Against the Wall

America? Sure, I like America.

I am walking home from the Columbia University bookstore on 116th Street in uptown Manhattan. It is dusk. I am clutching, in brown paper bags, some springback folders. Frank Kofsky's *Black Nationalism and the Revolution in Music* (with a sombre John Coltrane holding tenor sax on the cover), two Playtex dishwashing gloves (WITH EXTRA RIGHT HAND, AB- SOLUTELY FREE!) and some quarto-size unlined typewriting paper. It is cold. It has been sixteen, twenty, twenty-five degrees below freezing in New York for day after day: brown- grey ice frozen in cesspits around the street-corner lamp posts, discoloured by the fossilised dog turds disinterred by last week's thaw. At JFK Airport, where I was a few days earlier, the wind factor had reduced the cold to an unbearable twenty- one degrees below zero; between car door and heated air cargo terminal the skin stretched, froze, pained.

Tonight it is not that cold: to my son's delight snowflakes drift down and across beneath the streetlight glare, a gentle white litter across the pavement like the powder my wife leaves on the bathroom floor. They alight, explode, dissolve.

Car headlamps lift and slide down Amsterdam Avenue, heading for Harlem. I cross 121st Street. I am rugged up in Afghan sheepskin coat, six-foot scarf, gloves, black-woollen watchcap. I walk slowly, trying not to slip, down past the block of deserted buildings which Columbia University has pumped empty of tenants before razing it for a college of pharmacy. Three years ago they tried to build a gym around the corner in Morningside Park, which is a black haven, and the students took Columbia over. It was the first of the great American campus rebellions. But Columbia keeps on.

Only the liquor-store sign is alight. I don't need anything. But as I reach the doorway, its iron grille drawn back, I notice what seems to be a brawl going on inside: a black guy, and Max, the grey-haired store manager, and another guy. Forcing another drunk out of the store, I guess: it happens all the time. I have just enough time to wonder whether to get involved, and decide not to, when the store manager slips on his back onto the floor. The other two are standing over him. Both black. Max is a Puerto Rican. He levers himself onto one elbow. One of the men, a big awkward guy in a light corduroy jacket, slips a hand into his left pocket. In his hand is something dark, indistinct: a gun.

He points it down close to the store manager's body. Like all the stories say, it sounds like a firecracker. The manager's body bucks. Is it really happening? The men seem so clumsy, so vengeful. They back out of the store, shamblingly, not sure where to go. They look up Amsterdam Avenue and run past me, not very fast: big guy, jacket, short napped hair, twenty-five to twenty-six, six-foot three, burly shoulders, and a shorter, lithe guy in blue pants and maybe a black cap. They reach the corner of 121st Street, hesitate, wonder, finally turn and lope up 121st Street towards Morningside Park. The guy in blue is slightly in the lead. It is only as they round the corner out of sight that they begin running fast.

Inside the store the manager is on his feet. He is yelling, stumbling and falling around; his assistant, another Puerto Rican, is on the phone. I go to the door, walk inside. The manager has yanked his shirt out of his trousers. On the left side of his body, at liver level, is a neat round puncture mark. Blood is trickling down, undramatically, to his woollen underpants.

The assistant can't get the police emergency number. The manager grabs the phone, yells into it. I feel helpless, stupid. A young woman, fattish, black hair, runs in through the door and takes over the phone. 'He's been shot, yes he's been shot, for Christ's sake get an ambulance!' she shouts. I tell her the address, she hangs up, grabs the manager and forces him into a chair. Take it easy, keep cool, would you like a smoke? The shock is getting to him. He leans back, blood coming faster now, nodding his head from side to side and mumbling in Spanish. He wants to go to St Luke's. He's a Catholic.

Two uniforms appear. The Morningside Community nightwatch patrol: guns, nightsticks, black-leather uniforms. Where the hell were they? One of them, a thin black guy with drooping moustache, takes out a notebook, lays it flat on the counter, takes out his pen. Everything so painstaking. He writes nothing, says nothing. I look at him. His eyes are blank. He can't even speak.

Five minutes later, fast, the police arrive. A big Irishman, six foot, fourteen stone, wide pasty face. Questions, in a hurry, but unpanicky. What'd they look like? Jacket? Negroes? Height? Any cap? Where'd they go? The park, of course.

'He's been shot,' says the young woman.

'What?' says the cop.

'Didn't you bring an ambulance?' says the woman.

The cop gets on the phone, orders one, out the door again. Two more squad cars pull up, red rooftop lights swirling, swirling. Snow, people clustered outside. Can the manager describe them? I hit one of them, says Max, I hit him over the head with a bottle. There is broken glass, cheap whisky and blood on the floor. He wants to go to St Luke's. A cop from one of the squad cars comes in. Would you like to go in a radio car? Yes. They shoulder him out, feet first, the puncture hole as neat as ever, still not much blood. But it hit his liver.

An elderly woman comes in. The description she gives tallies with mine. She starts elaborating.

'I haven't got time for that now, lady,' says the cop.

Outside, the siren from the prowl car starts up. The assistant starts to close the store up: sliding the iron grille across the entrance, heavy-duty chains, two padlocks. The store has been held up seven or eight times in the last few years. Two months ago, the old lady who owns it had her wrist broken in a hold-up. This is the first time anyone's been shot.

I walk on home. Around the corner. Past the Eldridge Cleaver posters (Panther H.Q., dense black bullet holes in the shattered glass), the Karate and Soul Spectacular ads, FIGHT RACISM AND OPPRESSION NOW, clenched black-power fists, the faded election flyers (THERE IS NOBODY BEHIND JESSIE GRAY BUT THE PEOPLE), the boarded-up doors where kids sneak in to smoke grass, shoot scag. Up the snow-flecked pavement which curves rightwards towards the park. My wife is due to go to a P.T.A. meeting at Public School 125, directly opposite our apartment, that night. I take care to walk her across: simply, across the street. And back.

Probably professionals, says the Jewish professor who lives on the floor below me. Too old to be junkies. He's lived in the neighbourhood for years: a professor of literature at a city university, six-foot two, over thirteen stone, cross-country skier, boxer, comes from the south, has two rifles and a shotgun in his apartment. I describe the way the bigger man shot the manager while he was on the floor; a deliberate act of vengeance, it seemed, because Max was on his back, helpless. Or else the hold-up man lost his cool, shot him to get free, out the door.

Probably meant to kill him, says the professor. Less chance of getting identified. Probably murdered four, five people already. For a habitual criminal, half a dozen raps behind him, killing someone won't make any difference: it's twenty years, either way. The professor, he's moving to Chappaqua, in upstate New York. Suburbia. He doesn't scare easily. He's never been mugged. But his kids can't play on the street, and his wife carries a gas gun.

On the wall of our apartment, a brooding poster of John Coltrane. Dead at forty-nine. On the record player, Albert Ayler, the greatest of the avant-garde black saxophonists: dead at thirty-seven. They fished him out of the East River a few months ago. The violence isn't one way.

The hold-up men aren't arrested. The next day I go back to the liquor store to see how the manager is. He is in terrible pain but he should live. The owner is a seventy-two-year-old woman, frail, wrinkled, with gentle eyes. She is not smiling today. She's been held up so many times, she was going to close the store at the end of the month. Now she'll close it sooner. She's not rich. Yes, they took the money. But she'd always told Max to let them take it. Sometimes he'd wanted a gun; sometimes he hadn't. She would never let him have one. What was the money, compared to someone's life? If you got gun-happy, you never knew where it would end ...

She stops.

Wrinkled hands, wrung. Keys: she has to lock herself into the store, even in the mornings. You want something, she unlocks the door ... maybe. Mauve dress, hunched shoulders, no accent. Lined, once-handsome face weathered to a dry old leather. A New Yorker. I like her very much.

'This morning I was so full of hate,' she says, 'I was ashamed of myself.'

We live near 122nd Street, on the half-dozen blocks which separate Columbia campus from Harlem. 'Hell, that's way past the DMZ,' someone told me. Across the street is Morningside Park: 'Muggers' Alley', the cab-drivers call it. Sometimes they refuse to take me home. 'Won't go up there at night,' one of them told me. Said another: 'I got nothin' against 'em, it's wrong to condemn the whole race because of a few bad. But a pal of mine got shot a few weeks ago. Just four weeks ago through the head. And he was an ex-marine. Always said he could take on any hold-up man. He found out. I went to his cremation.' He stops, mumbles on. 'Can't see 'em half the time, when it's dark ...'

Race and violence: the twin themes which constrict the guilty heart of America.

Two nights after the liquor-store manager is gunned down, the little Puerto Rican delicatessen near 123rd Street is held up. Two men, both with guns. Then Jan's the boutique on 121st Street which the girl students from Barnard College go to. Gunpoint. The local shopkeepers get nervous, start closing dead on nightfall.

A day later, driving down 121st Street in my old VW van, I hear a woman screaming. It is three o'clock in the afternoon, broad daylight. A black guy sprints past, making for the park. A woman runs up: she's been mugged at knifepoint, robbed of her week's pay.

Same week. Evening. A teacher who lives on the second floor of our apartment building (he teaches mentally disturbed children, takes them to Aqueduct Racetrack for the day—'They like it') hears the noise in the street below. A man is levering open the boot of the old car belonging to the students on the top floor. He grabs a BB rifle, shouts, whips off a couple of rounds at the running figure. Exactly ten minutes later, high-pitched screaming from down Amsterdam Avenue. Another mugging: a black woman this time. I don't see the guy, but a police car which is prowling down Morningside Avenue suddenly stops, police empty out. In the clear, crisp night air the shots ring out: one, two, three—four. I can recognise them now.

The cops halt at the edge of the park, guns drawn, uniforms glistening in the eerie lamplight. They peer down warily into the tangle of bushes, brambles, blackness. The man is safe.

This is a fringe zone: Columbia students, Jewish shopkeepers, working-class Irish, welfare residentials, Japanese, Puerto Ricans, Chinese, blacks from the Harlem high-rises. Grimy New York apartment blocks, iron fire escapes disfiguring the outside walls, gutters choked with trash and snow-slush. Around here, most of the crime is committed by blacks. And most of the victims are black people, who suffer the violence of The Man and men: murder, brutal attack, rape, maiming. Except for muggings (armed robbery), which are mainly black against white: the ofays have more to offer.

At night the muggers come up through the park and hit the people 'on the hill'. A few hundred yards further up the hill, the bastions of American WASPdom: Riverside Church, Columbia University, the Cathedral of St. John the Divine. 'An Acropolis by day, a jungle by night,' the guidebook calls it. Same as Washington, D.C. I start off by thinking it is like living in middle of a guerilla war.

It is only slowly I realise I am out of date. America is under siege, and the war has already started.

Our children go to the local public school. P.S. 125. It's about 90 per cent black and Puerto Rican. Virtually none of the Columbia faculty send their children there; they get a subsidy not to. The week after our children started there a seven-year-old girl was raped in the school grounds. In school hours. I joined in the protest outside. Mainly black mothers, carrying signs reading GORDON MUST GO and GORDON'S BLACK, ACTS WHITE. The principal, Mrs Gordon, was black. The Parent-Teachers' Association had fought for a black principal, but when they got her they didn't like her. There was a series of emergency meetings. Another Harlem principal who had won a recent confrontation between the local commnity and the New York Board of Education, came and pleaded for Mrs Gordon ... because she was black.

'We got a revolution going on here!' he told the amphitheatre of parents at P.S. 125. 'We need what power we can get. I got nothin' against white people, but I got a lot against the enemy. And right now the enemy's white.' They listened, and they agreed, and they didn't take any notice. They got another principal. Black.

Our children like the school. They've learnt what it's like to be in a minority. They aren't colourblind. 'Why has that lady got a chocolate face?' asked our four-year-old daughter when we went to register our children. But they never use skin-colour to describe each other: it's always that girl in the red dress, or the thin boy who likes dinosaurs, or that boy over there near the rocks: 'I'm gonna marry him, he's got kissable lips.' Our pale blonde daughter found herself something of a favourite in kindergarten. The children kept stroking her long hair: just like Goldilocks. But by first grade the children had become more self-conscious, and began teasing her because of her freckles and because she didn't have an Afro.

That's how our four-year-old identifies everyone. 'What sort of hair does she's have?' she asks. She goes to the Morningside Park playschool, in the middle of the park. The two black women who run it, Gloria Lind and Bernie Grissom, take all-comers; the playschool is a beautiful mélange of black, white, Japanese, Chinese, Spanish (and Australian) children. No hassles. In the middle of Muggers' Alley. Something goes wrong somewhere.

Our kids' black friends are tolerant. And try to protect us. Coming up in the elevator with my wife one of them, Angela, turned to some cousins and said: 'See, I told you she was white!' Her cousins tried to hush her up:'It don't *matter* about that, Angela, it's what kinda person you are. People is people, it don't count what colour y'all are.' Later on, one of the elder cousins, embarrassed, took my wife aside. 'That Angela,' she said, shaking her head, 'That Angela, she's somethin' else.'

You got to be careful.

Guy we're sharing the apartment with, he's coming home one night and he does everything right. He parks the car, keeping the windows locked so no one can jab a knife through. He checks the street, sidewalk, entrance to the building. No one around. Locks car, checks outside stairs for crouched figures. No one. Makes fast for the lobby door. Unlocks it. Suddenly, running footsteps. Turns to check if it's a neighbour. It's a black guy who has timed it just right, sprinting over from hiding in the park. With a gun. Our friend yells for the building superintendent. He's smashed across the face with the gun butt, goes down. Wallet taken. He's found unconscious, face ripped open. Taken to hospital. Of course, he carries two wallets. One for the muggers, one for himself.

What does it do to a man, getting old, two kids, to have to carry two wallets around all the time?

The building is heavily armed. Nearly every apartment has a gun of some sort. The professor of literature, the big guy from the south, avoids the elevator: he runs down the stairs, rounds each corner with his head at surprise level, sometimes crouching, sometimes stretching, always checks the lobby before entering or leaving, walks against one wall or the other to the street. Checks through lobby panes for figures inside, outside. Walks at odd angles. He has a spring-lock, a chain, an iron-bar police lock and a steel sheet on the front door; an automatic timer to switch the lights on and off; a system of buzzing codes for lobby and apartment doors ... as well as the shotgun and two rifles. Like I say, he hasn't been mugged yet.

But then, I'm smaller than he is.

Our building is three-quarters deserted. Columbia University has been trying for years to tear it down, and the surrounding buildings. They got everyone out of one building and ripped it down; it's been a rubbish-strewn, fenced-off vacant lot for seven years. But a handful of tenants here stuck it out.

WE WON'T MOVE. It's the poster on the door of the woman in the apartment opposite ours: she is a fund-raiser for radical groups, including the Black Panthers till a few months ago. Strewn through the building in other apartments are some Columbia students, two black families, a Jewish rabbi, the professor, a woman social worker and her friends—and, on the ground floor, Juanita Kimble and her nine children. She is a squatter who moved into one of the empty apartments a year ago with the help of tenants, black radical groups and S.D.S. students: took on Columbia, the police, the Super, everyone. All the other deserted apartments—huge family places with four or five bedrooms each—are bolted, barred, sheet metal over the windows. The same with the surrounding buildings: one of them has a single tenant, an old woman. Columbia lets them crumble and rot away, waiting for the tenants to die off or get frightened and move away. The corridors are dark, grimy, and dangerous. A haven for muggers. Who are the violent ones, who the victims?

In the lobby, pinned to the tenants' notice-board, is a friendly notice from our local 26th Precinct police captain. His English isn't too good. This is what it says:

1. Try not to walk alone at night—have someone accompany you through the streets.
2. Have a friend or relative meet you at subway station or bus stop.
3. When you arrive at home, ring your bell to alert a relative or neighbour. Have a key ready in your hand to open door.
4. Don't enter an elevator with a stranger of any age.
5. Walk in an area that is well lighted—don't take shortcut.
6. Know the location of police call boxes and public telephone booths in your area.
7. If there are doorman in your neighbourhood know when they are on duty—they may be helpful.
8. Remain alert while walking. Look around you.
9. If you observe any person or group that appear suspicious do any of the following: (a) Use a police call box and call for assistance (b) Go to a public phone and dial 911 (c) If no phone is available, enter any store or residence and then call the police. Person in the neighbourhood are willing to help.
10. Try not to carry large sums of money, conspicuous jewelery or other valuables; when you cannot avoid this, secrete the cash and other valuables on your person—not in your wallet or handbag.
11. Don't place your house key together with other keys—keep

them separate. If you lose indentification papers together with your house keys someone may have access to your home.

12. Carry a whistle or a cheap battery-operated alarm that emits a loud buzzing noise when a pin is extracted. Those are sold in radio, 5-10 cent and department stores.

13. Carry your purse close to your chest. Don't dangle it loosely at arm's length.

14. If at any time of the day or night you hear screams or cries for help, pay attention—try to pinpoint their origin location. By helping your neighbour you help each other. Dial 911.

15. Do not answer downstairs bell unless caller is expected and known to you.

ACTION TO TAKE IF YOU ARE A VICTIM

● Remain calm—try not to panic. Very few victims of a mugging or a purse snatch are injured, if they remain calm.

● Don't resist or try to overcome a perpetrator.

● Study the perpetrator if you can. Note his description—height, build, approximate age, facial features, articles of clothing, etc.

● Call police as quickly as possible over police call box or public telephone 911. Remain patient.

● Notify the police in every case. Report of every crime are necessary to help us assign patrolmen where needed.

● Wait for the arrival of the police—don't leave.

● When arrests are made co-operate with the police and the courts.

THE COMMUNITY AND THE POLICE WORKING TOGETHER WILL REDUCE THIS PROBLEM

Every few nights the police stand near Amsterdam Avenue and pull drivers over to the kerb. Gypsy (unauthorised) cab-drivers, youths, carloads of Afros. Always black. Never white. Sometimes they're ordered out, stood up against a wall and searched. Harassment. The strong white arm of the law.

One night, walking down past the co-op, I notice a silver Italian GT sports machine edging the gutter. I walk closer. It's not often you see a Lamborghini in Harlem. A cop is leaning over it, the driver's papers. More harassment. The cop is white, the driver black. As the cop walks away I glance inside and realise it's Miles Davis. 'Hi, Miles.' Davis nods. 'I liked your last album, man.' Miles smiles warily. A blip on the accelerator, and the Lamborghini zloops out into the traffic and Amsterdam Avenue.

Miles Davis, the finest jazz trumpeter the world has known for two decades, used to play at a white-owned club called the Vanguard. There is no dressing-room for the performers, who are mainly black. You want a break between sets, you walk out onto the pavement. Miles did that one night—ended up being clubbed across the head with a cop's nightstick, blood down his face, thrown into gaol. Even Lamborghinis don't make a fat black cat safe.

One day the Super and some policemen arrest two Puerto Ricans on the roof of our apartment. They have ropes, break-and-enter gear. One of them turns to the Super, who is black. How can you do this to a brother? 'You ain't no brother!' snarls the Super.

The Super is a grossly fat, moody ex-army sergeant. He has a ferocious Alsation called Plato, a .45 pistol, a .38 Police Special, three Stetsons, a framed message from the Office of the President of the United States on the wall, and a smouldering sense of betrayal. He's typed out a primitive autobiography which reads like a parody of Erskine Caldwell: a blacktrash life of southern poverty, brutalised, degraded, threatened by white women wanting to seduce them a nigger boy. He escaped by joining the army; fought racism, fought Koreans, killed men, got to top sergeant—and was forced out of the service, he says, by a black major who told him one day: 'You a Tom, you always been a Tom, and there ain't no room for Toms in this army.'

He is a bitter man, and I am sorry for him. He gets drunk once a year, on Veterans' Day, when he marches in the parade. The One Day of The Year. He threatens to kill any intruder he finds in the building. One day, maybe, he will. Stickers on his car: National Rifle Association; Still Serving, U.S. Army Retired; the American flag. Prouder of his guard uniform and his medals than anything else. He indulges in long tirades against the Kimbles, the squatters, whom he regards as his worst enemies: they filth, they dirt, they defecate on the stairs and in the elevator, they got no right to be here, when they moved in that women called him a blackassed sonofabitch, a motherf——. He wouldn't repeat it. You think all those kids got the same father? He don't hate anyone, he don't care what colour anyone is, my friend, y'understand? But there is some people ain't hardly better than animals.

And then: 'You don't have to be white to be a pig.'

The guy in the radio shop up the street has an ugly knife scar down the side of his face, from eyelid to chin. Got it last summer. Tried to resist a hold-up man.

My car, a beat-up 1965 Volkswagen bus, is broken into four times in a month, stolen once. I notify the local precinct. Three weeks later I find it, myself, surrounded by junked cars down near the Hudson River, a few blocks away from the police station. I tell them, and they react fast: don't go near it till the stolen alarm is called off. Like, you want to get shot out of your seat by a police car?

Bob, the foodstore owner across Amsterdam Avenue, is a good-natured guy with a fine line in New York wisecracks. Jewish. When he and his pals get going it's better than a movie. One day he turns serious. He really loves this neighbourhood, he tells me. Everyone's so friendly. So many types of people. Been here twenty years, would never move. Of course, his home's in the Bronx. 'You could never live here,' he says.

Went away for the summer. Five months on the road, travelling around America. I find I miss New York. 'America!' says the friendly fat guy in the arts-and-crafts storefront in Berkeley. 'America stops just outside San Francisco and doesn't start again till New York.' Got back just on nightfall: George Washington Bridge, concrete loops and whorls, and then that long long expanse of the Henry Hudson parkway planing away along the riverfront towards Manhattan's dusk and smog. A glad sense of return.

Tried to find a place to stay. Four kids in the VW, exhausted and fighting. Not a vacancy anywhere. Hotels, motels, all full up. Reach a welfare hotel off Broadway. Four kids? Not a chance brother. For one night? He is suspicious, undecided.

OK, but you got to get out in the morning ...

It was my thirty-seventh year to heaven, woke to a cockroach-ridden room and smells of shit, death, despair. Slime over the walls, green and orange vomit in the communal bath down the corridor, the Spanish radio blasting in the room next door. People waste out their lives here. In the street drawn tight around mottled throats against a wind heavy with the threat of snow; black, cracked boots and pinched skin; my life in hiding ... They have nothing to look forward to. Neither love, nor redemption, nor rescue: nothing. No wonder, then, the greasy peepshow sex, dull insentient bodies propped on barstools at 123rd Street, housewives mumbling to themselves and twitching their heads from side to side on Amsterdam Avenue, junkies propped against the doorways of those shattered, barred and blinded buildings which Columbia has hollowed out like rind. Nothing. I walk by, but I am drowning.

We move in with a friend. He rescue us. But what about those who aren't?

The snow begins to fall. The children leave thin grey footprints behind them. The trees oustide the school rupture a colourless sky. Where you been? says Bob, the storekeeper. Yeah, we got your suitcases, it's OK, says Jose. Willie, downstairs, has grown an Afro. The kids move up one grade. Gloria Lind has kept a place for our four-year-old in the Morningside Park playschool. I am glad to be back in New York. I feel at home.

Harlem. Kids playing in the shattered debris of the Fifth Avenue playground, fenced off like a concentration camp. The centrepiece: a burnt-out fighter/bomber, relic of America's fight for freedom in ... Korea? Vietnam?

Telephone man, come to untangle the phone line from the dumbwaiter. Ex-GI, twenty-two years, black. 'Hey, man, those your kids?' staring at the tribe of black and white youngsters running wild through the apartment. He's into guerilla warfare: he's been trained for it in Vietnam, man. When it comes, the blacks'll hang on; whitey's gone soft. Two Bell Corporation supervisors arrive, one big, one small: Laurel and Hardy as Mafia heavies. Why've you taken so long? Why didn't you check back? Get your ass outa here. Downstairs the Super is is blowing his top: someone half-knifed through the dumb-waiter cord, coulda damnwell killed him. Behind his back, the telephone guy flashes me a V sign. I smile, walk away. Wondering.

Bad scene. I buy discs at the Record Shack on 125th Street, Harlem's main thoroughfare, sometimes talk with one of the guys there. This afternoon a tall, thin cat wearing ostentatious black shades stands behind me, sneering, listening in. Elijah fanatic? There is something indefinably threatening about him. I forget about him, but when I go to pay he sidles past and waits, deliberately, outside. For me? I walk out fast and make for the corner; he follows. I speed up; so does he. Across the street, where a bus has pulled up. The thin black guy starts running now, jumping in and out between the cars. He gets held up. The door closes, the bus pulls away. Trying to throw a scare into whitey?

Jazz afternoon, Harlem Prep. McCoy Tyner, Coltrane's former pianist; Yusuf Lateef; half a dozen other jazzmen. Afros, dashikis, turbans, African decorations, red-black-and-green Liberation symbols, everywhere a warm, hip confidence. People smiling, ready to get happy. I feel like an intruder: I seem to be the only white there. They notice, don't say anything. I go to make a phone call, and the woman behind the counter— Afro, rich heavy body, red dress—lets me in. Another guy comes up to make a call. 'You'll have to wait till the brother finishes,' she says. Brother? I look at her. She smiles, looks away. Could have been a slip. After a while you get used to calling everyone brother ...

Two years. After two years. I am utterly involved. We all are. We wouldn't want to live anywhere else—in America. Made friends, got involved in the playcentre, the school, the neighbourhood, the movement. My wife takes to walking through Morningside Park by herself: it belongs to the people, if the people don't use it they'll take it away. Either the muggers or Columbia. Nearly everyone we know is committed, one way or another: to politics, the school, Black Power, the neighbourhood, something, everything. I admire them. Here is where it's being worked through: in New York, in America, which means the world. The future, in microcosm, on 122nd Street.

It is mid-afternoon, and I am walking down Amsterdam Avenue. A siren starts up, an ambulance siren; I'm used to it, don't turn around. Then a tactical police force siren, those shocking whoops and hoots which sound just like Second World War air-raid sirens. The two sounds conjoin in bizarre counterpoint, bloody and irresistible. An ambulance screams by, hurtling downhill towards Harlem. It's from Knickerbocker Hospital. And there is such a terrible desperation in the sound, such agony and yearning, so unbearable a mixture of wailing and warning within the sirens, that suddenly I am crying. There, in the middle of pavement, like a fool, walking down Amsterdam Avenue towards 122nd Street, where I live, towards Harlem, I am crying. In the middle of the afternoon. Real crying. Not much, but crying. Crazy, isn't it?

1973

Popular Culture

6. The Road from Wigan Pier to Surfers Paradise

Standing in paradise, or was it Surfers Paradise, on the roof of the Broadbeach Hotel, with a wind blowing in from the bikini-littered beach, I was surrounded by the crooked fingers or was it question marks of the hotel's rooftop ventilators and Frank Moorhouse and Henry Mayer and the besuited bloke from F.A.R.B. (Federation of Australian Radio Broadcasters) and Professor Ned Polski from the U.S.A. who had delivered the keynote address, such as it was, this being a U.N.E.S.C.O. seminar on entertainment, and I was trying to argue that minorities were where the action was, using as my text Appalachia New Orleans Nashville Mississippi Oakland and of course the myriad sub-, counter- and alternative cultures of the Queensland/North Coast hinterland, even as I spoke the wind lifting and ferrying the words out of my mouth across the baking acres of terry towelling suburbia, the U.N.E.S.C.O. seminarians (some of them) listening and shuffling their feet, others down at the beach already, preferring carcinoma to culture...

The Penthouse, cruising, ideology, vicarious conflict and the stoned heavyweight Clown were to come later...

Culture is activity. It isn't a series of gilt-framed paintings on a museum wall or aluminium hard edges locked up in private houses; it isn't a row of paperbacks on a library shelf; it isn't a folio of sheet music by an aristocratic German romantic; it isn't even a piece of recycled junk sculpture in Hyde Park, or a Christo-wrapped piece of cliff face at Bondi beach.

At least, it isn't primarily that. Culture is not a product but a process. It's an ongoing activity by which particular peoples at particular times strive to comprehend and order their own lives, and in the process they create artefacts, relics and works of art which are sometimes the only evidence we have left to us of what those people did to make their existence meaningful. But it is a mistake, and one which bedevils a great deal of artistic debate, to regard these relics—including the contemporary ones—as constituting culture itself. There is something pretty weird, in fact, as others have pointed out, about a society prepared to spend millions of dollars on a Rembrandt, or a Jackson Pollock or a Fernand Léger but willing to spend comparatively little on its own artists who are actually creating at the time. The relics of, say, Periclean Athens are widely admired today, but the Athenians would not have made the mistake of regarding a collection of artefacts from past and foreign cultures as an adequate substitute for creating their own. This is not to belittle the achievement of a Myron or a Mozart, or to disregard the way in which contemporary art feeds off its own history; there is a case, which gallery directors such as James Mollison or Patrick McCaughey argue quite passionately, for trying to make a provincial community like Australia aware of what has been achieved by other cultures at other times. The mistake occurs when audiences come to regard such products as what culture is all about.

What culture is really about is something else. It means activity, involvement, a continual effort to create some new ordering or interpretation of the contemporary world. It means taking part in movements and traditions which may, as an end result, happen to produce abstract expressionist paintings or a rock opera or a kitchen pot or a community show, but which are more important as activities in themselves than what they produce. In a community such as ours, for instance, the widespread activity of painting—from kids and schoolchildren, to art students, to weekend painters, to full-time painters—is more important than any single painting it may produce. It is the scale of the activity, its widespread diffusion through the community, which counts, because in a democratic society that is the way in which people's lives are enriched and changed. To those who still hold to the overwhelming importance of 'great' art, one can point out that all such art springs from firmly established traditions and movements anyhow; a Shakespeare is the culmination of a vital and popular tradition of Elizabethan drama, not an historical accident, and his achievement would have been inconceivable without the theatrical culture which preceded and supported it . . . just as a Jesus, to change the parallel, came not to destroy the prophets but to fulfil them. I admire Richard Meale's compositions, but they are finally of less social and cultural importance than the extraordinary degree of music-making which goes on in our community: local choirs, chamber groups, symphony orchestras, amateur performances, eisteddfods, recitals, jazz groups, rock groups, country and western jamborees, a million people playing guitar and piano and recorder, singing their own songs, making their own music. Our culture, like our politics, should be participatory.

Society doesn't usually have to choose between pop/communal and élite/artefactual. Australia has a broad enough range of cultural activity to encompass both. It's only the politicians and arts administrators who have to make decisions about how much money to give to each activity; among such people the élitist approach is still so firmly entrenched that most public subsidies still go to safe, traditional activities (opera, ballet, painting) rather than to community groups who might challenge the status quo. As for the vexed question of 'quality' . . . Well, in some ways I feel sorry for those professional critics who have made themselves careers passing judgment on works of art, according to some floating standard of excellence (you get to see a lot of mediocre art and drink a lot of bad sherry). I've been a critic myself and I think good criticism is incredibly difficult and ultimately valid, but it has to be kept in perspective as a sort of ancillary to the actual process of creation. It can be argued, I think, that the quality of particular works of art can usually be left to history, time, and a slow process of differentiation. In any vigorous, creative endeavour the 'quality' will look after itself; it's the energy and dynamic of the activity which guarantee that the completed artefact will be worthwhile.

Once this view of culture is accepted, it becomes evident that one of our tasks is to take culture out of the hands of the 'experts' and to diffuse it as widely as possible. Fortunately the technology of the twentieth century has made this possible in a way undreamt of a few generations ago, and here I am thinking not merely of the mass media, such as radio and television, but of technical developments which have radically expanded the way in which art is created.

Let's take the Instamatic camera. As well as being cheap and therefore available to almost everyone, it has drastically simplified the matter of taking a photograph. Together with the new wave of automatic cameras, it has made it possible for almost anyone to take a good photograph, that is, to create good art. For themselves. For their families. For friends. And even, possibly, for a public audience at a photographic exhibition, camera club or art gallery. Whereas taking a photograph was once so complicated, and required such skill, that it was the province of experts and professionals, it is now a simple activity which turns everyone into a photographer. Even children, whose talent as expressive painters has never been doubted, can now create photographs which once might have required a Lartigue behind the lens. The perception, humour and formal construction of this everyday photography is often astounding; it's no wonder that some 'art' photographers have now begun to imitate and exploit these pop styles, even, in the case of leading San Francisco photographer Harry Bowers, throwing away his Hasselblad and reverting to a box Brownie to achieve simplicity and a commonplace authenticity of tone. Photography, it seems to me, is a good example of what a creative and dynamic art form should look like: an extraordinarily wide popular stratum which involves almost everyone in the community; another stratum of amateur creation which is nevertheless self-consciously artistic; and a narrower level of highly refined, highly sophisticated artistic achievement. In general, the photographs created in this last group will probably be of more lasting artistic quality, viewed in traditional terms, than most of the others, but they are not the justification for the entire activity. As I have argued, any widespread artistic activity, whether it be the taking of photographs, the singing of songs or the making of craft objects, is valuable for its own sake, whether or not it happens to produce highly developed art works. Also, it's clear that some of the most precious creations of our cultures—from Minoan figurines to West African masks to the Border ballads to the blues—are the products of a widely diffused popular activity. There is an obvious and direct parallel between such folk arts and contemporary mass arts such as photography. One has to be wary, therefore, of formulating an artificial distinction between the achievements of mass and sophisticated art forms, or the mass and sophisticated strata of the same art form; the 'best', though we may not recognise it as such until later, may be in the streets around us.

The same general argument, which I owe basically to Harry Williamson, the graphic designer, can be made about other technical developments such as the home movie, the video camera, the tape recorder and the photocopier. All of them have made self-created art possible for millions of people. Home movie outfits are becoming almost as simple and popular, though not yet as cheap, as cameras. The cassette recorder has turned every bathroom baritone into a recording star. Video has taken individual sexuality out of the bedroom onto the TV screen. The photocopier has turned every file clerk into a visual manipulator of the elements of chance, inspiration, originality and plagiarism. It has also made possible, as has the photo-reproducer, the mass production of art works which were once regarded as preciously unique. John Berger pointed out long ago that original art works, with their limited clientèle and inflated market value, should hardly any longer be regarded as valuable in themselves, when they can now be reproduced a thousand times over. The ultimate absurdity is the artist who deliberately uses a mass reproduction medium, such as the etching or lithograph, to produce a limited number of çopies—and then destroys the plates: There's artificial scarcity for you. As authors learnt long ago, it is not the individual one-off manuscript that is important, but its reproduction in a multitude of printed copies. Faced with this reality, the writers have learnt to be humble; the painters have yet to become so.

The validity of this emphasis upon activity is most clearly demonstrated in the performance arts such as theatre, music, opera and ballet, and communal arts which by their nature are spread through the community. What about more solitary arts, such as poetry? My own view is that in such arts communication is an essential part of the activity; 'poetry' includes the reading of poetry, just as 'theatre' includes performing for an audience. Though I write alone, I do not write for myself alone; the dissemination of literature and the act of reading are central characteristics of a literate culture. The act of writing is only the starting point of a complicated cultural process in which many people (writers, editors, publishers, critics, readers) are involved. Again, it is the process, not just the product, which is important.

The division which exists between élite culture and popular culture poses a dilemma for any contemporary artist. It can seem, sometimes, that you are faced with a choice between creating freely a minority art for a minority audience, and deliberately restricting and modifying what you create in order to achieve a mass audience. Neither alternative is really acceptable. If you follow the first path, as many contemporary painters, poets, composers and other artists do, you lend yourself to the conspiracy by which art, which should involve us all, becomes the property of a small, privileged and often powerful élite, thus perpetuating the artificial gulf between art and its rightful audience, the people. If you choose the second path and self-consciously try to create an art capable of communicating to a great mass of people who are unfamiliar with or untutored in art forms, you run the risk of creating art which is at best severely limited and diluted, and at worst hollowly propagandist and patronising.

Ideally such a choice shouldn't be necessary. In the words of Adolfo Sanchez Vazquez, the Marxist theoretician, the artist would then become someone who, in order to create for all men and women, on the one hand 'produces for a wide consumption or enjoyment of his product without giving in to the exigencies of mass consumption, and on the other hand ... maintains the highest aesthetic standards in his work, without reducing it to a creation for élites or privileged groups'.

Easier said than done. The essay writer, of course, does not escape the dilemma, and though I respond to much of what Vazquez argues (in his book *Art And Society: essays in Marxist aesthetics*) I think his conclusion, that the dilemma cannot be solved until capitalism and its exploitation of people have been abolished, is unnecessarily gloomy and too narrowly ideological. For a start, it tends to postpone strategies of action in the arts to some far-off, indefinite time when the whole of society will have been remade. I am not convinced that a radical change in the mode of production will *of itself* solve the questions posed by the relationship of the artist, art and audience in a mass society; there is something utopian about such once-and-for-all solutions. His conclusion also leads Vazquez into making unnecessarily rigid distinctions between minority and mass art and unnecessarily harsh criticisms of contemporary popular culture. He habitually refers to what he labels 'mass man' as hollow, depersonalised and debased. 'Truly popular culture does not exist in highly industrialised capitalist countries', he says, which is simply and demonstrably wrong. Elsewhere he says 'we can at least say ... that there is no relationship between quality and popularity'.

Now, one of the heartening things about contemporary popular culture is that there *is* a relationship between quality and popularity. It is no accident that the best songwriters of our time, namely the Beatles and Bob Dylan, were also the most popular—immensely and unprecedentedly popular, with their work taken up, played, sung and listened to by literally millions. Tony Palmer, music critic for the London *Observer*, once described Lennon and McCartney as the best songwriters since Schubert. If what some Marxist critics argue is correct, they wouldn't have won the largest audience; some nameless hacks in an ad agency would have instead. The same holds true in other popular arts, such as cartooning, or even films; the very best artists are also among the most popular. Quality doesn't necessarily condemn you to a minority audience, though it may tend to push you that way. As I will point out in the following essay in this book, the deciding factor is often the stage of development reached by the particular art form you are working within. It is much easier to solve the dilemma I have been discussing if you are operating in a medium such as film, which still combines 'high' and 'popular' roles, than in a medium such as poetry or jazz, where the degree of sophistication and refinement has pushed it to the point where it has become a minority art.

People also rework and make over, in significant ways, the materials supplied to them by a heavily commercial culture. There are probably more parodies of the current crop of TV beer commercials than there are commercials. Successful exploitation films such as *Superman* and the *Star Wars* saga depend upon a certain amount of self-parody; they know they will never be taken seriously, even by the most gullible of audiences. Art which attacks or satirises the established culture can become so popular that it is sometimes promoted by the very people who, in theory, should attempt to censor it: look at punk rock, early-to-middle-period Dylan, late Lennon, the American sick and black humorists, Feiffer, Scarfe, Hunter S. Thompson (at his best), Allen Ginsberg, film makers such as Peter Watkins, critics such as John Berger—the list is endless. The popular arts keep evolving new genres and forms, or new directions in old forms, which the commercial culture is forced to take notice of. It's obviously in the interests of that commercial culture to manipulate, distort and finally annex the new movements; it tries to do that all the time. But it rarely succeeds in destroying such movements completely; they have a habit of resisting, changing, and then breaking out in a new guise. The divisions within the mass media and in the established culture are so great that they can never present a united front anyhow; it's not uncommon for elements of the mass media to be highly critical of one another and to be engaged in promoting and defending conflicting interests though in Australia, of course, the concentration of media ownership limits this.

I believe it is essential that those opposed to the system create not just optional cultures, as in the various alternative lifestyles, but an oppositional culture. If we use the mass media, technology, creativity, or whatever to evolve our own culture, with its own values, beliefs, stances, ethics, etc., it can't help but be opposed to the dominant culture of our time. But that opposition needs effective forms. Hence the importance of developing countervailing media and institutions, and the necessity, in Australia especially, of using these quite purposefully to break the media cocoon which contains us. 'I might say it, but I don't really believe it', one highly successful newspaper editor told me when I argued (in print) that the responsibility of journalists was not to the owners of news-papers but to the community at large. Well, the time has come to believe it as well. The airwaves, the radio bands, the TV channels, belong to the people, not to a small band of ogilopo-listic entrepreneurs. In any sane society the major means of communication, including the print media, would be made responsible to the community, to the people who use them and need them, not to those who simply seek 'a licence to print money'. Lord Thomson and Rupert Murdoch are relics of a nineteenth-century system of values; they should be put in a museum.

Vazquez is right about the social nature of art and the pri-macy of communication in the artistic process; he rightly op-poses the idea of art as mere self-expression. 'Art is essentially dialogue, communication, an open sea in time and space', he says, and argues that art is social not only because it is created by a socially conditioned individual but also because 'it sat-isfies both the creator's *and the consumer's* need for expres-sion' (my italics). He has some very valuable things to say about the cause and nature of alienation. And he defends, correctly, the achievement of art (Aeschylus, Cervantes, Shakespeare, Goethe, Balzac) in societies which were basic-ally hostile to it, and the need of artists to create freely and not conform to the demands of social realist, propagandist or Stalinist art. He is a bit harsh, perhaps, on folk art, or what he calls 'folkloric' art; he seems to regard it, in an old-fashioned way, as intrinsically inferior to more refined art forms, as though it were merely a preparation for what was to follow. There is the faintest hint of élitism about his unstinting praise for the Great Artists of history, and the way he seems to ignore the movements which created them; but perhaps he is redressing a (Marxist) imbalance there. Towards the end he reiterates the maxim that all people are artists, and that in an ideal society there would be no 'painters' but, at most, people who engage in painting, among other activities. Certainly all people are creative; as a teacher, one of the most heartening experiences of all is to have this confirmed, and to realise that it is only necessary to find the right medium to tap the enor-mous potential which people have.

Watching a film of kids skateboarding one night, I was struck by the intensity, the sheer human dedication, of it all. It was pervaded by a sense of celebration, like a modern version of a pagan ritual of life-renewal. South London kids, these, skating in a concrete bowl gouged out of dirt on a vacant lot surrounded by tenements (urban renewal?); not T.S. Eliot's old women gathering papers, but a pride of young people, bent on heroism, achievement, fulfilment. In a different social system, perhaps, all that human potential might go into politics, or at least into some channel of communication which allowed society to benefit from and respond to such inputs. Instead it's channelled, apolitically, into sport. The same applies to surfing. Or Aussie Rules. The parallel with art is clear. It is not the creative resources of people that are lacking, but the sort of society that would make these qualities manifest.

What we must do, three-quarters of the way through the twentieth century, is to create our own culture for ourselves. It's too important to be left to others. One of the grim realities of our time is the way in which the mass media, which are controlled by a very small group of people, dominate our culture. Television, radio, films and newspapers have turned many of us into passive receivers of culture instead of creators, or have attempted to. What they pump at us, as we slump before the telly, is highly commercialised and highly manipulative. We are bombarded almost every hour of our lives by advertisements and advertisement-related programmes which try to induce us to act as the media controllers and advertisers wish us to. It is instructive that the man from F.A.R.B. (Federation of Australian Radio Broadcasters) at Surfers Paradise talked about the ability of programmes 'to deliver an audience of so many hundred thousand to the advertiser'; in a commercial society we become so many units of consumption to be delivered, trussed and bound, to the sellers. The messages we receive are also highly political. Use of the media is one of the ways, perhaps the crucial way, in which the controlling élite in our society exerts its hegemony; the media both consolidate and expand this hegemony, and persuade us every day that 'this is how it should be'. In Australia, in particular, where just three media chains control most of our TV, radio and newspaper outlets in a way which would be inconceivable in Britain and illegal in the U.S.A., the influence of this media barrage is immense.

What we should do, instead of simply receiving this culture (and its concealed functions) is to create our own culture which reflects *our own* interests instead of the interests of those who want to manipulate us. In that way we have a chance of freeing ourselves, and, though the task is difficult, it is not impossible. Beneath the superstructure some alternative culture often runs true. The great mass of people does not, I think, totally and unreservedly accept the given system, no matter how people may be frightened, bribed or manipulated to vote at elections. In popular discourse the overriding doctrines of the existing system ('free enterprise', 'private initiative') are most typically derided and ridiculed. People, in their own lives, often live out alternative or resistant or hostile values. It is by strengthening this resistant culture, understanding it and endorsing it with our actions and responses that we help counteract the power of those who would try to manipulate us into submission. A popular music tradition, for instance, which is based upon the practice of forming your own bands, writing your own songs and making your own music inevitably acts as a countervailing force to the established culture. There have been attempts, more successful in the U.S.A. than in Australia, to set up countervailing media: FM stations, video centres, cable TV, public broadcasting, alternative newspapers and magazines, populist publishers.

Some parts of the media are freer than others. Cartoonists such as Bruce Petty and Tony Edwards, the one operating through traditional media and the other through alternative media, can express in their work a view totally opposed to the dominant social/political ethos. Comic strips and black-and-white art generally can do the same thing. So can films, though the cost of film-making often compels the involvement of commercial interests; video makes it easier. Graffiti, broadsheets, pamphlets, demonstrations, marches, strikes, protests . . . all help. The politics of the Australian people has always been more radical than is reflected in the media or the biased electoral system.

All this hardly needs restating, except that occasionally you get critics niggling away at the apparent hated him/loved her paradox involved in liking the people of a nation, but being critical of the political and social superstructure which imposes itself, like a parasite, upon the backs of those who actually make it all work. There's no paradox there. You like people, but you're aware of the way in which the social structure of the community they live in bends them. It hangs together. If you *don't* like the people, then you're really in trouble; it's but a short jump (or drift would be more like it) from a dislike and distrust of 'the mass' to the sort of turncoat élitism of a Paul Johnson, former editor of the *New Statesman*, or the mass-murder paranoia of a Stalin.

People, the great mass of humanity, have much in common; you either like them, whether you happen to be living in Australia or Vietnam or Poland, and you're on their side, no matter what political system they exist under, or you should give up any claim to being part of the Left. 'We ought to drop an atom bomb on the place,' a Sydney Trotskyite, talking about New York, said to me once. It so happened I had just returned from living for two years in New York, and had come to realise that most people there opposed the system which exploited them, and many of them had involved themselves in techniques of opposition which Australians were not to copy until years later: urban terrorism, mass protests, neighbourhood co-operatives, squatting, radical movements such as black power and women's liberation, and armed resistance to police and politicians alike. It is sometimes in the heart of the beast, as Che Guevara recognised, that the greatest commitment, and courage, and personal morality are displayed.

What are the chances of developing a real, popular resistance to the dominant ideology and culture of our time? At an informal level, as I've said, this resistance goes on all the time. Australians often display a lovely scepticism about the given culture which surrounds them. Unfortunately, they rarely go further; it's as though the perception itself were enough. It isn't, of course. Over the years I've come to realise that the only safe and permanent way of combating the dominant ideology is to embody our opposition in structures, institutions, movements, parties, social experiments—the whole panoply of formal (as well as informal) resistance. I'm aware of the dangers inherent in institutions and structures, the way in which they can develop into self-serving power centres in their own right, but that is just an extra complexity which the Left, and people generally, have to deal with on the road back from Wigan Pier. To be specific: this means developing and working through political parties such as the Labor Party, and through such mass movements as the trade unions, co-operatives, the women's movement, and the liberation movements (sexual, black, unemployed); breaking down the mass media chains and expending a great deal of energy on creating alternatives; and making a profound overhaul of our educational system, which at present hardly ever questions the ideology it perpetuates. It also means pushing through radical initiatives in the law, the constitution, the electoral system, parliament itself, financial institutions, tax, the welfare system, the means of production, exchange and distribution—in fact, the entire range of what are usually considered socialist initiatives and principles. It means reversing the way in which power, like water, at present flows from the top down instead of from the bottom up. The mass media should not, for instance, signify manipulation *of* the mass but manipulation *by* the mass. That means taking over the media and making over our culture. Though the mass of the people does not at present have the power, it has the numbers. In a democratic system it should, eventually, win through.

Before the U.N.E.S.C.O. seminar ended, I flew back to Sydney. A rock opera was folding under my feet. Against my will, it had been depoliticised, emasculated, turned from Brechtian tragedy into pop farce. The problem of reaching a mass audience with uncompromising, highly political art remained. But at least, standing there watching my words sprinkle like confetti amid the sociologists and F.A.R.B. people and Hawaiian Tropic bodies of Broadbeach, I was convinced still of one thing: culture is activity . . .

1982

7. Pop Goes the Culture

Melbourne. Whew! I am howling down the Geelong freeway, the semis pass like gods, the You Yangs are smudged Williamscapes behind the right lobe of my mind, I am listening to Matt Taylor's 'I Remember When I Was Young' on the cheap pushme-pullyou radio with the built-in buzz and . . .

'LOVE IS WHAT IT'S ALL ABOUT!' Unquote, Swamp Dogg, songwriter. Thank you, Swamp Dogg, thank you, Matt Taylor, thank you Mississippi Fred McDowell, bluesman. Hot. This is where the bushfire jumped the road that time, burned out four cars and seven people. Or was it eight? You keep moving, you die; you stop, you get killed all the same. They catch you once, just once off base, Papa, thank you Papa with the twin 12-gauge muzzles thrust down your throat in hypersexual retribution . . . nevertheless, thank you Papa thank you Swamp Dogg thank you thank you . . .

Axiom 1 Pop is energy. Rock is energy. Movement is energy. We are all energy, we are part of the Heraclitean stream, we are moving in blowfly trajectories from creation to death and as we hurtle along this invisible airborne stream we try to conjure up images symbols correlatives which correspond to this sense of speed tragedy and joy, and we create music. And if we are twentieth-century people, we create the blues, and then jazz, and then swing, and then rock 'n' roll, and then rock—all of them the creation of an oppressed, alienated race of ex-slaves who thus provide for oppressed, alienated, post-industrial man (no accident this) his pervasive pop music. 'I do not play no rock 'n' roll', says Mississippi Fred McDowell. (I found him on the sidewalk once, near Seventh Avenue in Greenwich Village, playing slide guitar with his begging hat, an upturned bowler, on the concrete in front of him.) He was wrong. Already white kids all over the world were playing slide guitar like this old black man with the half-Chinese face, singing the same songs, borrowing the same rhythms, calling it rock 'n' roll. The media work so fast, pop cannibalises its own folk sources while they are still growing. Fred is dead now, but his music is alive and well.

Axiom 2 Pop is new. Nobody ever played blues guitar like Robert Johnson played it until Robert Johnson played it. Nobody ever heard that sound before. Contemporary pop, the blues-based music which has now saturated Western culture and become both its most trivial and most important art, is genuinely new. All art, especially popular art, is social: it reflects/crystallises/reshapes the society from which it springs, and behind Robert Johnson's two-finger treble-string A7th chord shape lie three centuries of Afro-American cultural history which is synthesised in this single, authentic sound. The world had never heard that music before, because the world had never experienced that culture before. And so one man's cry ('All of us had a type of cry in our voice') becomes a symbol for us all. And yet, at its black/white/yellow core, a paradox. 'Y' play de blues, y' play de blues *away*, y' unnerstan'?'

Axiom 3 Jazz is hot. Rock is hot. Pop is hot. I am driving down this white-slotted tar-bumped heat-crimpled road to my death, I am grave-bound and breath-bled, but I am metamorphosed (metempikehoses); all I hear is a shout of joy! The century turned over like an old woman, and from out the rotting funkybutt south burst music that had at its black heart a lament that was yet a shout of freedom. *Great Gawdalmighty, free at last!* Thus the paradox, to which we unthinkingly respond: despair/joy, slavery/freedom, resignation/affirmation. It was a unique but unprecarious fusion which singed flappers' ears in the Windy City, turned Bix from keyboard to Salvation Army cornet, rolled across America and then the world of the Jazz Age and spawned the first authentic genius of modern popular music, Louis Armstrong. In the span of one man's clenched fist, growth from archaic to classic art. Amen, Pops.

We needed you. And within a generation the same unlikely fusion of tragedy and ecstasy (trad theatre masks, Painted Black) had become the Invitation To The Dance of our entire culture: black bottom charleston jitterbug jive shake rattle and roll twist funky chicken frug watusi boogaloo stomp bump disco and other Dionysian rituals of celebration.

Axiom 4 Pop endures. You fly high, you play the chord, you do the thing, and the waves vibrate out through the black air of the universe indefinitely. The sound and the act, once done, are indestructible. Are you listening, Father? Are you listening, Big Bopper, down below? Art persists. Pop art persists informally (usually), orally (folk), instinctively (graffiti), traditionally (jokes) and sometimes media-transformed (Beatles). All art forms are originally popular, refine themselves eventually into minority forms. Halfway, sometimes, they face, Janus-and-Joni-like, both sides now, become both popular and high art: theatre (Shakespeare), the novel (Dickens), film (Ford), pop songs (Dylan). The conjunction is ephemeral: as the form is refined, becomes more sophisticated, the audience dwindles. Sometimes there is feedback from élite art to the mass audience (*Mona Lisa*), but it is atypical. Play it again, Sam.

Sometimes, of course, we stumble, lose heart, fall and retch by the tarmac. *I am locked up in this white room, baby/I am lying on a mattress listening to the radiator hiss/I can't move, I've lost you/get to your feet/you're on the road again/I wish you everything/you want your life to bring* (punctuate to taste: everyone's life as a pop song).

Axiom 5 Love is what it's all about I believe you, Swamp Dogg, I believe you, Father, I believe you, Krishna, I believe I believe I believe

I think

I think I believe

Zap! Transformation, transmogrification, transubstantiation. Where am I? Why, I am in the pub, I am sitting alone in the back bar with a packet of salt and vinegar chips, a glass of Carlton draught, feet propped on a chair, backed up against a slops-wet butt-ugly laminex table winking at the old lady with the rolled-down hosiery who says am I awright mate yes I'm awright luv and watching the local hips in 1930s gowns and sharp midriffs and zippers and listening to the jukebox pumping out Matt Taylor Stones black funk 'Knockin' On Heaven's Door' and suddenly *Zap* right there, in the pub, in the back bar, EPIPHANY: of course, you should always listen to pop on a jukebox, or at a dance/disco, or on the road at 110, because it is not simply itself (though it is that too) it is an environment, it is an envelope for survival, it is an objective correlative for twentieth-century subjective life . . .

Well, for a pub epiphany it wasn't bad. Music as environment. Art as living. Rock as a life-assist. Pop as a raft between instants of experience. That sort of thing . . .

Well, I remember when I was young
I had a sometime love
Who never knew it
Well, I'd do tricks for her on my bike
But it never turned out right
I always blew it . . .

It is hot. T-shirt sticks to my back. Kids squawling a bit. Whew! I am howling down the road to my death but I am transfigured, I have music in my blood in my mind in this my insubstantial soul, I have been given life and I have given life back, I have nothing else to ask; I am completed. LOVE IS WHAT IT'S ALL ABOUT. Thank you, Swamp Dogg, thank you thank you . . .

Let me put this another way.

The dominant culture of any society at any time is its popular culture. It is not intrinsically separate from the 'élite', 'aristocratic' or 'high' culture (all unsatisfactory terms) of any society, though aristocratic societies such as those of the Enlightenment perpetuated an artificial separation between the two; hence the growth of the romantic image of the Artist as Outsider, dissociated from and even opposed to the general contemporary culture.

In his *Notes Towards the Definition of Culture*, a quintessentially conservative text, T. S. Eliot defined British culture in terms of 'a Cup final, the dog races, the pin table, the dart board, Wensleydale cheese', etc. The culture of any community is contained in forms and rituals and activities, from wedding ceremonies to sports to sex habits to entertainments, which we create to give shape and pattern to our lives and thereby make them comprehensible. Understandably, it is this mass or popular culture which most clearly reflects the nature of the society that spawns it. You look hard at American football, for instance, and you see a perfect reflection of the brutality, wealth, sheer professionalism, racism and emphasis upon power of America itself. Similarly, if you want to understand Australia and the lives Australians lead you must turn to bush picnics, Anzac Day, the Melbourne Cup, surfies, backyard barbecues, poker machines, Sunday in the car and all the other rituals of Oz pop culture. The culture of a community determines to a large extent what it feels like to live there, its peculiar flavour and way of life. In Australia, especially, it is pubs rather than play-readings, sex-roles rather than symphonies, which give life its characteristic ambience.

Sometimes these activities shade off into art. Dancing, for instance, is a social activity which changes from culture to culture, adopting characteristic forms in each: the polka, the rhumba, the can can, twist, disco, punk. It also changes from generation to generation: compare the cool, mannered formalism of the waltz (although it was originally regarded as daringly lascivious) with the hot, anarchic, self-concerned qualities of contemporary dance styles. But dancing is also an 'art', ranging from genuine folk forms (flamenco) to urban pop forms (disco) to highly refined 'classical' forms such as ballet. Indeed, a characteristic of many popular arts is that they perform a functional role as well as an artistic one (though I am not trying to draw a clear distinction here: the two interfuse). A dance, as I have said, can be a social ritual and an art form at the same time. A cartoon or an animated film, such as Bruce Petty's, can have a political and an artistic function. Popular arts such as comic strips, posters, snapshots, pottery, craft work, etc., often perform a multitude of functions. This is no criticism of them, necessarily; one of their strengths can be their functional character, which may protect a pop art against the etiolation, rarefication and isolated self-concern which can afflict a 'high' art.

I don't like the term 'high' art, but for the purpose of this essay it will have to do. High arts are not necessarily *superior* to popular arts, but they are usually more *refined*—more sophisticated, more highly developed. This refinement tends to give them certain admirable qualities such as subtlety, imaginativeness, complexity and profundity, but it can have its drawbacks, such as loss of energy, obscurity and lack of immediacy. When people talk of the high arts, they usually mean the traditional, established arts of a cultured minority within the community: drama, literature, painting, sculpture, 'classical' music, ballet, opera. All of these have a long and illustrious history behind them. They are high arts in the sense that they are highly developed, highly refined, and have a high (in the sense of high-quality) artistic achievement behind them. The case for the 'high' arts hardly needs restating, and my own sympathy for the popular arts goes hand in hand with a long involvement in the traditional arts.

What is often not understood is that all high arts develop from popular arts. Classical music (the sonata, symphony, tone poem, concrete/electronic assemblage, etc.) did not spring fully formed from the foam, nor even from the brows of church and baroque composers. It developed originally from the folk musics of the common people of Western Europe, and in early classical music its folk origins are perfectly clear. Indeed, successive classical composers have returned to folk idioms and styles for their source material. Similarly, contemporary painting is the product of a long tradition of folk art which began with cave and bark paintings, evolved through various ritualistic, popular and communal forms, and even today makes periodic returns to primitivist (e.g., West African) and pop (e.g., advertising) sources. All high arts are the result of a similar process. We need to value our popular arts, therefore, partly as the seed beds from which all our arts have sprung.

What disquiets the cultural élitists in our midst, however, is not the populist beginning of all art (a historical fact which even they do not care to contest) but the fact that this is a continuing and dynamic process, and that energetic popular forms can rival and supersede established 'high' or 'classical' disciplines. They don't like the idea of a continuing (cultural) revolution which perpetually challenges the established order. We don't have to look far, however, to see examples of popular arts superseding established disciplines. The novel is a comparatively late arrival on the literary scene; it began as a popular entertainment, a picaresque low-caste yarn, and within two hundred years had become the most important literary form in Western culture. The film began as a box of tricks for diverting children and novelty-seekers; today it is a mature and demanding art form with its own cinematic tradition, its own history of 'classics' and its own high artistic achievement.

But perhaps the best example is jazz. In the short space of fifty years it transformed itself from an archaic Afro-American folk music to an intensely sophisticated high art which has refined itself to the point where it has lost forever the mass audience that gave it birth and supported it through most of its development. Jazz, in fact, presents in a compressed and contemporary form the case history of how most arts develop. Every art springs originally from the generalised popular culture of a community, in this case the work songs, dances, parades, laments and church rituals of black Americans. It evolves popular forms, some of which may prove to be ephemeral (minstrel music, ragtime), others of which prove to have the resources and formal qualities necessary for further development (the blues, spirituals, New Orleans 'jass'). As the art develops still further, it reflects both its popular character, through the influence of its history and its popular audience, and the increasing refinement and creativity of the artists who are involved in it; it becomes both a popular art and a high art at the same time. This occurred with jazz in the 1920s, when it was a popular dance and listening music and yet was being forged into a formidable expressionistic art by an authentic genius such as Louis Armstrong. By this time jazz was a high art in the sense that, through the creativity and ambition of gifted artists such as Armstrong, Jelly Roll Morton, Sidney Bechet, Duke Ellington and others and through the continual honing by a wide range of participants which occurs in any vital folk or pop art, it had been brought to the point where it was capable of creating enduring masterpieces which reflect the maturity of the form itself and which rank with the achievements of other major (but much older) artistic disciplines. The exact parallel in English drama is Shakespearean theatre, which appealed to both popular and minority culture audiences; in literature the parallel is the late-nineteenth-century novel and the work of authors such as Dickens, who reached a mass audience through his serialised novels for an indisputably high art form. In our own time we have seen the same thing happen with the film, which, in the hands of directors such as Ford and Hitchcock, has been a mass art and a high art simultaneously.

It is perhaps when an art form is being sustained by its popular traditions and yet is reaching out for new and daring achievements that it typically creates some of its greatest work: Elizabethan theatre, the Victorian novel, and classic jazz of the 1920s and 1930s sustain that argument. The conjunction of popular energy and self-conscious artistry seems to release an enormous imaginative burst of achievement within the tradition. But even as this occurs, the art form is usually being transformed from a genuinely popular art into the art of an élite minority; the conjunction between the two cannot be sustained for long. The reason, of course, is that, once an art achieves a certain level of sophistication, it cannot usually retain a mass audience. The form has reached such a stage of specialisation that only a highly educated, highly knowledgeable audience is capable of appreciating and understanding it, and a characteristic of our society is that we do not try very hard to educate the mass of people to that level, or to bring them, by whatever means, to that degree of awareness. It may even be that, by the time an art has been stretched to the point that Charlie Parker brought jazz to, only a minority will be capable of responding to it. Whatever the case, the fact remains that as the art refines itself still further, its audience dwindles and it becomes more and more the preserve of a small, highly cultured minority. This is exactly what has happened to poetry, to contemporary 'classical' music, to avant-garde visual art . . . and to jazz. The serious contemporary novel shows signs of going the same way.

Unfortunately, the art form is then often identified with the social class which has the leisure to pursue and appreciate it; it becomes a 'highbrow' art for 'highbrow' or 'aristocratic' audiences. Poetry, quite wrongly, has suffered this fate, hence the attempt of some self-consciously popular or vernacular poets to rescue it. One of the possible responses of an art form to this crisis is to split itself into 'high' and 'commercial' forms. Thus, though the commercial novel and the commercial film may still reach a mass audience, their high art counterparts reach only a small one and serious novelists in Australia now find it impossible to make a living from their art, a position with which the poets and many composers have been familiar for a long time. To return to jazz: An art which began as a popular music, achieved a mass audience, and became the staple pop music of the Jazz Age is today an avant-garde minority music with a minority audience and all the characteristics of a high Western art. One could hardly have expected anything else: the trajectory is typical, symbolic and perfect.

Today, it seems to me, rock music is going through the same process. Here is a new popular music which, in an incredibly short time, has become the dominant music of the Western world. By dominant I don't mean 'best'; I mean that, through sheer popularity, rock has overwhelmed most other pop musics and outstripped most other pop arts. And, if the trajectory I have described for other arts is valid, we have not seen anything like the end of its development or its artistic attainment. The process is being speeded up by the media revolution, which force feeds twentieth-century art to an early maturity. The novel took 200 years to reach a formal apogee; jazz did the same in fifty years; rock is trying to do it in a couple of decades. It may even in our lifetime perform the complete transformation from pop origins to high formality, from chrysalis to butterfly, to final inanition, moth dust blowin' in the wind. Whatever the outcome, it's a fascinating process to be involved in.

What we are witnessing today in rock is the emergence of a genuinely new art form ... It is the focus for a fantastic amount of creative energy; it is expanding, moving in a dozen different directions at once, cannibalising everything from folk to country music to rhythm and blues. It's a hybrid, but then so was jazz. In fact, the similarity between the current rock scene and the Chicago jazz scene in the 1920s can't be just accidental: there is the same frantic competitiveness, the same swapping around of musicians from group to group as bands break up and reform every week, the same bizarre names (Canned Heat equals Jelly

Roll Morton's Red Hot Peppers) and ingroup sex titles ('Ballin' the Jack' equals 'Back Door Man'), the same drug culture, the same hectic certainty that something is happening, this is where it's at. It's not just the scene that's the same: it's the stage the music has reached. Chicago was where jazz was formalised and rock too is now reaching out for sophisticated structures and forms . . .

from *Up Against The Wall, America*

I wrote that some time ago. Today I'm not so sure; at the time rock seemed to possess endless creativity, there seemed no limit to what it could achieve. The parallel with jazz still holds true, however, even if rock doesn't end by achieving an equal complexity or artistic maturity; the history of art is full of brilliant beginnings which stopped short of their potential achievement. And, if nothing else, rock has given us the best popular music the world has ever known.

This needs some explanation. First, it needs to be recognised that most contemporary popular music—rock, soul, blues, reggae, jazz fusion, boogie, gospel, disco, ska, funk—is genuinely new. It has virtually no precursors in Western culture. It is fundamentally a 'hot' music which provokes a 'hot' response; it is derived not from the mainstream of Western culture, from European sources, but primarily from the African music which black slaves took with them to the New World. In the United States this fused with other influences to create a unique Afro-American culture, that of the black American, and a series of unique Afro-American musics. The current pop scene represents the latest triumph of the black 'hot' concept over the predominantly 'cool' tradition of European music; a triumph which is confirmed by current substyles such as disco, punk and reggae. Although these later styles, especially disco, have been thoroughly commercialised, reggae and disco began as minority black musics and punk, though it is basically a white English style, represents a reversion to the 'hot' characteristics of rock 'n' roll.

What does 'hot' mean? The term was invented by black jazzmen shortly after the turn of the century. In his book *Shining Trumpets* (which remains the single best sociomusicological introduction to jazz), critic Rudi Blesh has included a six-page chart analysing the 'hot' concept and its derivation from African survivals in black American music. In summary, it means a way of singing and playing which generates excitement and emotional intensity by using a whole range of Negro techniques: complex rhythms, hypnotic beat, clipped notes, 'dirty' tones and dissonances, blues inflections and an intense, taut delivery. Stevie Wonder, Sly Stone, Aretha Franklin and James Brown, for instance, are hot singers most of the time, just as Cliff Richard, Neil Young, Frank Sinatra and Engelbert Humperdinck are cool ones. Elvis Presley started off hot but quickly cooled down. The Beatles went the same way. Louis Armstrong played a hot trumpet; Miles Davis (in his cool period) and Chet Baker were stone cold. It's easy to hear, feel, experience the difference. Today many rock groups, from the Rolling Stones to AC/DC to Thin Lizzy to a myriad west coast, British and Aussie rockers, hold to the 'hot' concept, whereas soft rock European groups such as Tangerine Dream and The Moody Blues drift into cool pastel tones. As a rule of thumb, black American groups tend to be hotter than white European groups—the more substantial the infusion of white 'classical' sounds (e.g., Rick Wakeman), the cooler the result. Unfortunately, Marshall McLuhan got the terms 'hot' and 'cool' completely arse-up in his celebrated *The Medium Is The Massage* and other media analyses, reversing the meaning usually ascribed to them; he has paid the penalty of watching the terms revert to their original (musical) meaning. Don't mess around with the oral tradition, man.

The 'hot' concept has been gradually taking over popular music since the 1920s, when 'hot jazz' swept away the lingering remnants of Victorian and Edwardian music and inspired a dozen dance crazes from the Cakewalk to the Charleston to the Black Bottom which, in the context of the times, were as uninhibited as disco dances are today. By the late 1930s the big bands and their hot riffs had swept the pop scene and frenetic teenagers were jitterbugging to Tommy Dorsey's equally frenetic 'Well, Git It'. But it wasn't until rock 'n' roll arrived in the 1950s that the final conquest of pop music by the 'hot' concept began. Based on the black urban rhythm and blues which had been developing in American cities, especially Chicago, since the great migration of southern blacks to north American cities began in the 1930s, with doses of black gospel and white country and western music thrown in as well, rock 'n' roll represented the injection into the pop scene of the most archaic and fertile of all Afro-American music forms: the blues. Nearly all the great early singers—Little Richard, Chuck Berry, Fats Domino—were black and most of their songs were made-over blues. Singers such as Bill Haley and Elvis Presley were basically whiteface imitations of the black style: Elvis's very first record, 'That's Alright, Mama', is almost a note-for-note copy of the original by Arthur 'Big Boy' Crudup, a blues shouter and electric guitarist from Mississippi. The evolution of rhythm and blues into rock 'n' roll into rock is now exhaustively documented; the thread that runs through all the permutations, however, is black—and hot. Through his music, the black American has liberated the young people of the Western world from the typically unemotional, self-disciplined tradition of their own culture and given them a much more expressive one of his own. Hot music creates a fierce, physical reaction in the listener; it makes you want to get to your feet, move your body, clap, dance. It is a vital, extrovert music which aims at excitement, emotion, even exaltation. And good rock music, like good jazz, can reach a pitch of intensity and emotion where the only possible response is a shout of joy.

The dominance of rock can partly be explained, therefore, by the sheer quality of the music itself. It was a blast of rebellious truth in a music scene characterised by sentimentality, cliché, escapism, and the vapid work of Tin Pan Alley tunesmiths; little wonder it was taken up by young people as a symbol of defiance. Rock music itself, however, quickly succumbed to the lures of commercialism and showbiz exploitation, until today much of it has merged indistinguishably into the Top Forty middle-of-the-road pop much beloved by teenyboppers, parents, Eurovision Song Contests, Drake-style radio programmers, Molly Meldrum, and, of course, the entire music establishment which likes to *control* its product, not be controlled by it. Most pop music is junk; that is the inescapable fact that forces itself into your eardrums if you listen long enough. And yet that's more or less what you'd expect of any popular art: an immense amount of activity, a zappy but random vitality, and, at its best, real artistic achievement. In the work of artists such as Bob Dylan and the Beatles, rock has created popular art as great as any that has been seen this century in any medium.

But there are other reasons for rock's pre-eminence. One of them is the revolution in electronic media (McLuhan got that one right) which has made music the most easily disseminable of all the arts; in the age of the transistor radio, the tape recorder, the record player and the amplifier, music is everywhere. When the print media held sway, the printed ballad was one of the most popular of all art forms; as Edgar Waters points out in *The Literature of Australia*: 'In a time when there is no popular audience for verse, except the verse of pop songs, it is hard always to keep in mind that less than a century ago there was a mass audience for poetry.' Kipling was read all over the English-speaking world; Banjo Paterson's *The Man From Snowy River* sold out in a fortnight; C. J. Dennis's *The Songs of a Sentimental Bloke* sold 60,000 copies in eighteen months. The invention of the radio and the record player transferred this mass audience from poetry to pop songs. Today a bard such as Bob Dylan gravitates naturally towards the song rather than the printed poem, though the distinction between the two is becoming blurred. In a way this is a natural process, a harking back to original forms, because most poetry, in most cultures, has been sung. One could argue that it was the long-lasting ascendancy of the printing press which distorted poetry from its typical sung form to an atypical printed one: the pop song has restored it to its rightful format.

The hegemony which the United States media, from films to records, have over the rest of the Western world helps explain why it is an American style of music, rock, rather than Italian accordion music or German beer-drinking songs which rules the airwaves. New York's Tin Pan Alley has always had an inordinate influence on the world's pop music. But there is more to it than that. The growing ascendancy of U.S.-based media coincided with the rise of powerful ethnic minorities through the American social structure, and it is these ethnic minorities which, as I have argued in the case study of hot music, provide the source of most contemporary pop music.

Now, to understand this process it's necessary to understand the way in which the popular music scene feeds off regular infusions of 'non-commercial' or 'minority' music, and the way in which apparently new art forms such as rock—or jazz—are very often the product of minority folk arts which become popularised. In his book *The Jazz Scene*, the English jazz critic Francis Newton (who is also the social historian Eric Hobsbawm) has described how the evolution of jazz occurred parallel to the emergence of other major popular arts: the British music hall, the Parisian cabaret and the Spanish flamenco. 'The second half of the nineteenth century was a revolutionary period in the popular arts everywhere, though this has been overlooked by those orthodox observers of the arts who are snobs,' writes Newton. 'Thus in Britain the music hall separated from its parent, the pub, in the 1840s and 1850s. By general agreement it reached its peak in the 1880s and 1890s, which also saw the startlingly rapid rise of that other phenomenon of working-class culture, professional football. In France the period after the Commune produced the working-class *chansonnier* and after 1884 his culturally more ambitious bohemian derivation, the Montmartre cabaret . . . In Spain an evolution strikingly similar to that in America produced the *cante hondo*, the Andalusian *flamenco*, which, like the blues it so much resembles, appeared as a professionally transformed folk song in the "musical cafes" of Cadiz and Seville, Malaga and Cartagena, from the 1860s to 1900s.' And he comments, 'If I had to sum up the evolution of jazz in a single sentence, I should say: "It is what happens when a folk music does not go under, but maintains itself in the environment of modern urban and industrial civilisation."'

If you substitute 'rock' for 'jazz' in that second passage, you have a very good description of how a rural folk music, the blues, was transformed in the United States into an urban minority music, rhythm and blues, and finally into a mass or popular music, rock 'n' roll. The commercial music scene needs these regular infusions from outside because normally it lacks the vitality to generate significant new music itself; it can only process or merchandise someone else's. The infusion might come from jazz (hence the trad jazz boom of the 1960s) or folk music (hence skiffle, calypso, folk-rock), or Latin American music (bossa nova) or the music of the West Indies (reggae), or anything else. The entertainment industry processes and commercialises the new music as quickly as it can, diluting and softening it to make it appeal to as broad an audience as possible, adding everything from singing strings to watery lyrics, until finally it has drained the new music of all its flavour and made it virtually indistinguishable from the other commercial pap which is the staple of the industry— whereupon Tin Pan Alley looks around for a new shot in the arm to revive its flagging energy. Sometimes, as I have indicated, the transfusion comes from outside the U.S. The West Indies provided calypso and then reggae, Latin America has provided a whole string of dance rhythms (samba, conga, cha-cha, bossa nova), and more recently Africa has been the source of Afro-rock. But the prime energy source has been America's own racial and regional minorities: the Mexican-Americans of southern California created chicano music, the French-Americans of the deep south created Cajun music, the fusion of Appalachian mountain music and western prairie songs created country and western. Most significant of all, America's black minority, in a remarkable burst of creativity, had injected an astonishing succession of 'new' musics into the mainstream: jazz, blues, ragtime, boogie woogie, rhythm and blues, gospel, soul and rock 'n' roll. The pop scene feeds off these minority musics, which it popularises, commercialises, makes more 'sophisticated' and ultimately debases, and in the process it ensures that the energy generated by black Americans as they follow the Irish and the Jews up the American social ladder feeds the trannies of the world. No wonder rock is ubiquitous.

All art, especially popular art, is social. It is drawn from a specific social environment which it both reflects and shapes. Pop music is a particularly direct expression of this environment because of its immediacy of creation and lack of formality. The sound doesn't come out of a vacuum: the music is what it is because the society is what it is. If you look at three forms of contemporary popular music—blues, country and western and jazz—you can see this process very clearly.

The Blues

The blues is one of the great popular creations of the last 100 years: a *form* which, like the sonnet, seems capable of infinite variation and development, and a *feeling* which can pervade everything from uptempo Chicago rhythm and blues to avant-garde jazz. This is not the place to attempt a detailed analysis of the blues. What is absolutely unique to the blues, however, and what has made so many generations of people respond to it so powerfully, is its synthesis of sorrow and joy—a paradox which would be almost inexplicable if we were not aware of its social evolution. The sorrow that characterises the blues is derived from black slavery and the work songs, laments, shouts, hollers, arwhoolies, spirituals and moans which were synthesised in the blues form towards the end of the nineteenth century. The linear descent is complex but obvious. But the blues can also be joyful, a fierce act of affirmation in the face of tragedy: as so many blues singers have explained, they sing 'to sing the blues away', and those interlocked emotions can be heard in the voice of every major blues singer from Bessie Smith to B. B. King. And, as Wilfrid Mellers has argued in *Music In A New Found Land*, in creating the blues, the black American has created a perfect artistic metaphor for modern, alienated man. Writes Mellers:

> [It] began as the music of a minority. This minority, having nothing more to lose, could accept its alienation and its isolation for what they were, with a desperate fortitude denied to the members of an ostensibly prosperous society. Yet in so doing this minority could imbue its awareness of dispossession with a universal significance, making its melancholy serve as a symbol of the alienation of modern, urban man. D. H. Lawrence said that humanity today is 'like a great uprooted tree'; and James Joyce made the hero of his modern Odyssey a Jew. The American Negro was literally uprooted from his home . . .

The reason that the great mass of people have responded so instinctively to the blues in one or other of its forms is that they have found in the music of a dispossessed, alienated, ex-slave race the exact expression of their own dispossession, alienation and industrial slavery. Yet they, too, seek a way out. And so in a modern blues such as B. B. King's 'That's Why I Sing the Blues', which reached the top of the American charts, there is a yearning, and yet an optimism, an excitement, which we all respond to. It is our music that he is singing.

Country and Western

'Each of us had a type of cry in our voice,' says Roy Acuff, the country and western singer, trying to explain why Hank Williams was so phenomenally successful. *A type of cry.* It's this, more than anything else, which still gives country and western music its emotional impact. Those high, plangent tones, the nasal whine, the overt sentiment and familiar folksy themes—however much they are debased and diluted, there remains at the core of country music a cry of loneliness which, though it sometimes merges with the blues (Jimmie Rodgers' 'Blue Yodels' are a good example) retains its own emotional individuality. It is a cry which began in the southern mountains and backwoods of the United States, where 'hillbilly' music originated; in the words of folklorist Alan Lomax, 'the Non-Conformist revival exacerbated the moral and emotional conflicts of this Calvinist and patriarchal folk and touched all their music with melancholy, while their free-and-easy life as log cabin dwellers and marginal farmers gave their songs a tang of wildness and abandon unknown in Britain and the north'. Since then, the music has been steadily debased. As the settlers (and their songs) spilled out onto the western plains, their music merged with the western songstream and Nashville, Tennessee began its long climb towards becoming Music City, U.S.A. Jimmie Rodgers, the first country and western star, still retained much of the plaintive colour of the southern mountains, but in Hank Williams' singing it had become sentimental and stylised and in Johnny Cash it has disappeared almost entirely. Yet it is to the country tradition that so many contemporary singer-songwriters, from Dylan to Kris Kristofferson to James Taylor to John Prine, have turned for inspiration: they tend to be bards, storytellers, and their music is coloured by melancholy. Groups such as America, The Band and Crosby, Stills & Nash use those high, nasal harmonies in much the same way as the original mountain singers used them. A song such as Crosby, Stills, Nash & Young's version of 'Carry On' or 'Woodstock' belies its optimistic words; theirs is a music of dark-edged melancholy, of dolour, of a desperate and profound fear for the future. It is the alternative tradition in rock, the white, high-voiced, harmonised, Appalachian-European yearning for a transcendent peace, an incessant reaching after the infinite. When a modern rock group wants to express that emotion, it turns instinctively to the sound which, derived from a different social source, creates a similar feeling. In America, the right music is always to hand.

The New Jazz

The new jazz, as it's still called, is one of the most important developments in jazz of the last decade. The musicians who have been playing it—from Albert Ayler and Ornette Coleman, through Cecil Taylor, Pharoah Sanders, McCoy Tyner and Archie Shepp, to Roscoe Mitchell and others—are all black and politically aware. (In contemporary America it is impossible to be black and not to be involved, in some way or other, in the black struggle for freedom.) Their music tends to be neurotic, despairing, edgy, hyper-violent; it is the music of revolution and it sounds like it. The revolution, in this case, is both social and musical. These are sophisticated, highly intelligent, mature artists, often with a formidable background of music theory and composition—Archie Shepp, for instance, is probably an intellectual first and a musician second—but much of their music stems from a deliberate attempt to break down the old forms, patterns, chord structures, rhythms and conventions of the jazz that went before them. It is basically 'free-form' jazz, so much so that it often dispenses with set chords and set rhythms altogether; the musicians improvise by relying on an instinctive feel for each other's music. This 'freeing' process is a direct musical parallel to what these musicians are striving for politically.

In evolving this new jazz, these musicians have also tried to create a more communal music in which the emphasis is no longer on stars (soloists), or on forms which are dictated from outside (set arrangements), but on the group feeling which the band, as an embryonic community, can develop. They have consciously returned to older forms of jazz, such as traditional New Orleans jazz, where group polyphony and free improvisation were more important than solos and carefully structured arrangements. As jazz has done before (notably in the 1950s) this represents a conscious return to the roots. Once again, there is an obvious parallel with the black political movement and its emphasis on black roots and what is uniquely black: hence black pride, black is beautiful, Afros, black slang, black gear, black power ...

Jazz is a minority music; but as I have already argued, the minorities are where the action is. Even as sophisticated and comparatively formidable a music as the new jazz has had an effect upon the pop music of our time. The typical tonalities and sounds of the new jazz were picked up first by jazz-rock groups, and then by black soul musicians such as James Brown, and finally by white groups such as Tom Scott's L.A. Express. What the white teenager in Melbourne may respond to, ultimately, is a high, wild cry of protest by a black revolutionary in New York. Once again, perhaps, the music of a minority is on its way to expressing the unvoiced aspirations of a majority.

The achievements of popular culture should tell us something about that majority: their creativity, their energy, their imaginativeness, their fundamental artistry. It should force the élitists and aristocrats in our midst to revalue *the people*, and their unexpressed potential. Culture isn't just an artefact; it isn't just something we respond to, or are moved by, or gain an intense experience through—though good art can do all that. Nor is it just a handy way of getting at the structure of society, using it as a sociological tool—though it can be used for that as well. Culture is what we are all about. It is a crystallisation of what we feel, what we want, what we fear, what we live for. We shape it, it shapes us, it both reflects and determines our being, it is the way we try to understand and give meaning to our lives. Our culture is us.

Let me put this another way.

Axiom 1 Pop is energy. Rock is energy. Movement is energy. We are all energy, we are all part of the Heraclitean stream, we are moving in blowfly trajectories from creation to death and as we hurtle along this invisible airborne stream we try to conjure up images symbols correlatives which correspond to this sense of speed tragedy and joy and we create ...

1976

Oz

8. What's Wrong with Barry Humphries

So Barry Humphries is back on stage again, waving his gladdies, cracking his racist jokes, pillorying pinkos, aborigines, unionists and, of course, women, whom he seems to loathe, presenting his show *An Evening's Intercourse* (joke) on the Australian club-and-theatre circuit, endorsing washing machines, and generally doing his famous Dame Edna drag queen impersonation.

I admire Barry Humphries, always have. He's an extraordinary artist to have emerged from deepest Melbourne suburbia, an acid and forgiving commentator who long ago realised that Australian life was a marvellous subject for satire and deserved a good boot up the freckle—to use one of Les Patterson's lovely slangwords. It must have been a hard and brave thing to do in the early days, when the voice of the censor and the philistine was heard loud in the land; the fact that Humphries is now so popular—not only in England, but with the very targets of his vitriol in Australia—says something for the maturity of the average Oz audience, as well as Humphries' part in making it wake up to itself.

When I went to see his show at the Twin Towns Services Club at Tweed Heads, on Queenland's Gold Coast ('It's not a Town, it's a virus ... so central ... you can hop on a plane and in twenty minutes be somewhere interesting!' says Edna) I was overwhelmed yet again by the sheer theatrical power of Humphries' creations—especially Sir Les, Canberra consultant on The Yartz, who may be (as some critics maintain) a dated Whitlam-era parody in origin but retains enough brute tribal force to be instantly recognisable as the Great Australian Yahoo, still extant.

What worries me about Barry Humphries, however, is the fundamental source of his art. It seems to arise from a deep and abiding contempt for the human race, especially the commoner and the least fortunate members of it; hence what Professor R. F. Brissenden has called 'the bleak world of Barry Humphries' satiric vision'. This is not to deny his prodigious creativity, nor the acuity of his ear. But the stink of that fear and loathing pervades a great deal of what Humphries does, from his early freaks-and-pornography compilation *Bizarre* to the crude spit-and-shit-and-toxic-shock deluge he poured over his gullible customers (Aus$14 a ticket) the other night.

'Fart in their faces, Brian; serves 'em right for being on time!' Les Patterson orders a late arrival at the show, dribbling down his powder-blue crimplene safari suit, brandishing the right hand glove with which he has been 'sorting out the sheilas from the shirt-lifters' at the Commonwealth Games. From the start of the sketch Humphries hawks and spits at his audience, as though intent on immediately degrading them. 'I think there's almost a total hatred of Australia in Humphries' work. He's a satirist who loathes Australia and everything about it,' playwright David Williamson told me once. Right. But Humphries' detestation seems to extend to a lot of other people and groups as well.

For a long time he's got away with it because we assume that the racism and sexism and crypto-fascism which spews forth is not his but that of the character he is portraying—an old and ambivalent stage game. But what can one make of the fake newspaper placards with which Humphries delighted his largely Queenland audience:

BOONGS' TOOLS DEFINITELY LONGER

BONNER HOLDS HIS PIECE

KANGAROOS DEMAND TRIBAL RIGHTS

Hoots of laughter from the whites. Not much satire there. And almost every character Humphries trotted out displayed, unnervingly, the same racial sneers: at 'this little yella bugger', and the Hongkong tailor 'like a shark with jaundice', and the childbirth pain of 'tinted women who aren't as brave as we are', and Greek men who apparently play with their balls, and, from earlier shows, Bob Hawke and his Jew-boys, and those yellow bastards in Dixon Street, and ABO FILMS, and yellow velvet, and so on and so on and so on...it might be funny for Humphries, living in what his programme-note is pleased to called the 'austere luxury of his Estoril unit in his beloved Portugal', but for marginal people who live on the razor-edge of white prejudice and violence, it's serious.

It's possible that Humphries is simply parodying the characters he has created, yet there is a worrying ambiguity. Why the reiterated racial slurs, the racist jokes? If innocent, they nevertheless provoke cheap sniggers at racial stereotypes; if not, they coldly add to the immense sum of racial hostility everywhere. After a while it's clear the audience is just laughing at the racist jokes Humphries is dishing up to them— and, as usual, he is pandering to their taste.

The same worrying syndrome can be seen in Humphries' constant pillorying of the Left. We know that this is not just his caricature technique at work, because what happens on stage jibes so well with Humphries' own political stances. For instance, Lance Xavier Boyle, the Roman Catholic trade union secretary of A.C.U.N.T., and a feature of the current show, is presented as corrupt, phony, a two-timing charlatan. And in his recent book *A Nice Night's Entertainment* Humphries reveals the depth of his real feeling about such people:

> While performing him ... it was amusing to scan the stalls and pick out the pious pinkos gazing up ecstatically at the unsavoury opportunist on stage. Their poor little pinched faces always fell most entertainingly when they realised that the odious operator on the boards was one of their own sacrosanct self-sacrificing trade union lefties. [Pinko? That's a strangely outdated word to use, with its shades of McCarthyism ...]

Les Patterson is a Labor figure, of course; he was Minister for Shark Conservation in the Whitlam government. Humphries uses him to poke ribald fun at Australian Labor Party people: Bob Hawke: 'I wouldn't piss in his ear if his brain was on fire. No worries!' Don Dunstan: 'He's bipartisan.' Al Grassby: 'I knew him when he was a colour consultant for Darrel Lea.' The man behind Phil Philby films is a Leftie. So, I suppose, is underground film maker Martin Agrippa, who these days, according to Humphries, would probably be teaching at some deplorable university with its staff of 'lapsed Methodists and pious, root-faced Marxists'.

Humphries' own personal politics, I assume, is somewhere to the right of Ronald Reagan and Genghis Khan. He's on the editorial board of *Quadrant*, a conservative, right-wing magazine. For years now in his writing and statements he has heaped contempt upon the idea of 'social relevance'in art, and upon intellectuals, artists, academics, film-makers, feminists, protestors, unionists—and anyone else who wants to change the status quo.

He appears to be bitterly opposed to government grants to the arts, which he attacks in all sorts of ways, from his latest programme-notes to earlier caricatures like Brett Grantworthy—though some years ago, when his career fell upon hard times, Humphries himself applied for and was helped with a grant. Maybe he thinks all artists could and should hawk themselves around the advertising agencies and, like Humphries, star in advertising campaigns for washing machines, handbags, etc. (The programme-note lists as sponsors the manufacturers General Motors Holden, Perrier Water, McWilliam Wines, Oroton, OPSM Spectacles, Nivea Products, and Red Tulip Chocolates.) Such is the adulation given to Humphries by much of the media that on his last visit to Australia one newspaper was reduced, in its search for an original slant, to writing about Humphries The Businessman—and mind-boggling reading it made too!

The trouble with Humphries' profound political bias is not its right-wing extremism but the way it distorts his satire. In an Australia which had a Liberal/National Country Party government for seven years, and which is characterised these day by tax-evasion scandals, take-overs, business manoeuvres, government corruption, recession and phantasmagoric resources booms—all of it, one would think, rich material for satire—Humphries is still trundling out Whitlam-era figures, old targets, and warmed-up Edna leftovers from the 1970s. There's not a single new figure in Humphries' show. No businesspeople, no media personalities, virtually nothing about comtemporary Australia (except for a few stray references to Malcolm Fraser and Brian Maher). Where the hell has Humphries been in the last few years, except in Portugal? Certainly not living in Australia.

It's interesting that one of his most sucessful and enduring creations, Sandy Stone, is a dealer in sheer nostalgia. In this latest show he has 'passed away' and is living in a sort of St Vincent de Paul heaven; apart from a lot of tasteless stuff about 'maximum security twilight homes' and 'Rent a Stiff', his memory for the impedimenta of the past is perfect and endearing: pianola rolls, rupture trusses, a Morphy-Richards toaster, Namco pressure cooker, half a jaffle iron, Fowlers Vacola bottling outfits, quinces and clingstone peaches, the top Colac orchestra ...

But it's hardly of our time.

As well as all the other things he despises, Barry Humphries seems to despise women. The women he picks out of the audience to drag up on stage seem to be nearly all fat and pliable and hence easy objects of ridicule. His characters include Joylene, who has a rape whistle around her neck and keeps blowing it but hasn't managed to get raped yet; and another female who grows sprouts on used cotton wool—'You can get toxic shock from her alfalfa.' In his book he defines *feminist* as 'a woman, usually ill-favoured, inclined to chemise-lifting'; a *chemise-lifter* is 'a female invert or daphne' which in turn is connected to *shirt-lifter*, ('poofter, a male invert'), and, I suppose, *pillow-biter*, ('one of the new breed of forward-looking Australian art-museum curators').

Dame Edna, however, best encapsulates Humphries' hostility towards females; it's surely no accident that his most famous creation is an arrogant, philistine, emasculating bitch who is a bundle of the very worst characteristics of stereotyped womankind. In the current show Dame Edna has been stripped of virtually any satiric content, and, far from being a parody of the everage Oz suburban housewife—which was her original role—she is now something much closer to Humphries himself: namely, a globe-trotting 'mega-star', as she calls herself, who clearly detests her audience, heaps insults upon it ('I mean that in a nice way'), sings rude songs about *My Public*, and concludes patronisingly that there's no difference between them except 'You're down there and I am up here.'

Dame Edna, like Humphries, has made it; on the Gold Coast

she was wearing a satin knickerbocker suit, gold trinkets, high-heel satin shoes, and a brand new blue rinse, and she exuded opulence ('I'm so so grateful, it's a marvellous feeling'). It didn't make her any more loyal to her sex: one woman's dress was described as being like a 'turtle-necked pantyhose', there was much hilarity about an 'intimate women's op' and another hapless audience participator was labelled a 'manic depressive'.

'Humphries always attacks his audience, he likes to manipulate them and demonstrate his power,' says someone who knows his work. In the first section of her show Edna babbled on endlessly about what a star she was, to the point where she was not just a Drag Queen but a drag. In the second half she pulled four women and a man out of the audience and got them to cook and eat a barbecue on stage—not an intrinsically humorous situation, but one which allows Humphries to boss his victims around like naughty little children. 'I'm making this all up as I go along. I wouldn't insult you with a rehearsed show,' Edna declared. For once, she seemed to be speaking the truth. The services club clientèle laughed, unbelieving.

It's possible, as some people suggest, that Edna has developed a life of her own; or, as others maintain, that Humphries and Edna are no longer distingishable. (If you spend a large part of your life dressed as someone else, that's understandable.) Either way, I am left with this awful vision of a man struggling to rip a mask off his face which has grown into his flesh; or, worse still, who is *not* struggling.

Edna ended her show with her traditional gladioli giveaway, ordering her obedient front-rowers to tremble their phallic gladdies. As the curtains closed, she thrust her bejewelled hand through the gap and gave a final two-finger up-your-crotch sign, which seemed an appropriate symbol of her attitude to her audience.

One should keep in mind, however, that Barry Humphries is very, very funny. His timing and stage panache is superb; in the course of the show I noticed only one joke which fell absolutely flat, and that was piece of nasty bigotry about Roman Catholics. A young couple behind me were almost hysterical with laughter. They especially liked Sandy Stone's stuff about death and roast beef, and how twilight homes always have 'an old boy in the next bed with his mouth open', and the neighbour with his eye on Beryl's cumquat, etc. There were some genuinely perceptive pieces of observation, such as his description of widows with their freckled elbows poking out the tourist-bus windows, 'their hubbies' watches on their wrists'. But of real satire there was very little. Much of the show was taken up with the sort of crude sexual jokes, song-and-dance acts, sight gags and Old Dame pantomime humour which wouldn't have been out of place at the old Tivoli; he came across less as a master caricaturist than as a stand-up-knock-down music hall comic.

What satire there is (and God knows these times deserve satirising) seems to spring more from Humphries' personal obsessions and political biases than from the social involvement and responsiveness one would expect of a great satirist. As Bob Brissenden points out in his introduction to Humphries' book, his caricatures are presented as 'lonely, shallow, selfish, vulgar and vain'—and with a certain degree of malice. The London *Daily Telegraph* has called Humphries 'as aggressive as he is compassionate', which shows just how little it knows about Australia and the true nature of Humphries' art. Aggro he certainly has, but he displays about as much compassion as, to use his own phrase, 'a half-sucked mango'.

In his programme-note Humphries calls himself 'widely liked'. But I don't know anyone who actually *likes* Humphries; they admire him, perhaps, or laugh at him, or are wary of the deep cynicism of his work. But *like* him? He's good. He's funny. He's got a great ear for the idiosyncratic inflections of Australian speech. But there's something missing: some largeness of heart, some sense of purpose or perspective, which might have turned his work into something approaching greatness.

Years ago, when discussing Humphries in *People, Politics and Pop*, I wrote: 'I have long suspected that Barry Humphries' particular brand of satire, brilliant and entertaining though it is, is rooted in a profound anti-humanism'. Revisiting his show, that disturbing quality is more evident than ever. And whereas I once thought that creations like Neil Singleton might develop into full-blown, three-dimensional characters, it's obvious now that Humphries' art has remained frozen at the level of the cardboard caricature.

A great artist, even a great satirist, needs some sense of perspective which we can vouchsafe our allegiance to. You don't have to be a Leavisite to recognise that any artist who is crippled by a distorted and uncompassionate view of the human condition is likely to create a minor, limited art which we distrust. Perversely, instead of satirising the great and powerful and famous, the traditional and deserving subjects for satire, Humphries turns the full bilious force of his contempt upon the losers and defenceless in society. Abos, Jews, migrants, unionists, feminists, the great mass of common people, are mere subjects for scorn. If any victims dare rise up and defend themselves, he seems to be up there with the rich and powerful kicking their heads in.

Humphries' art is profoundly reactionary. It reminds one of nothing so much as the grotesque and despairing cabaret which flourished in Berlin as the Nazis began their terrible climb to power—a resemblance which is emphasised by the song-and-dance routines with which Les Patterson and Dame Edna end their acts. At best, Humphries is habitually on the wrong side. At worst, he is dribbling and spitting his way around a club stage, cracking dirty jokes, spouting bile and banalities, marvellous and funny still—but, as I've said before, just another clown.

1982

9. Return to Awfulville

Nobody, it seems, likes suburbia, except the people who live there. Barry Humphries, Patrick White, a succession of visiting planning pundits and of course those glossy architects who advocate high-rise, high-density living, all have had a go at suburbia at some time or other. Australia is probably the most suburban nation in the world. Over three-quarters of the population lives in cities and towns, and most of them live in those sprawling acres of red brick, double-and-triple-fronted bungalows, each set on its own quarter-acre block, which you drive through for an hour before you can get into or out of any of Australia's major cities. I must admit I have some reservations about suburbia: about the cultural poverty, and isolation (especially for women), and lack of services, and social distress suffered by many people who live in the outer suburbs, to say nothing of the sheer drag of travelling long distances to and from work and the exclusion from many of the things (excitement, entertainment, interaction with people, the whole panoply of urban culture) which make life in the city worthwhile. You live in Penrith, or Blacktown, on the far western outskirts of Sydney, and you must wonder whether you're living in the city at all, and whether it wouldn't be better to move off to the bush or a country town. A lot of people have done just that.

And yet, in defiance of all the shouting and haranguing from town planners, architects, politicians and councillors about the advantages of high-rise, high-density living, most Australians persist in demanding a suburban bungalow set on its own block of land. They like it. And in order to get it, apparently, they are prepared to live further and further away from the city centre and to suffer all the disadvantages that entails. Of course, the bureaucrats try to coerce them. As Hugh Stretton writes in *Ideas for Australian Cities*, new urban developments are often distorted by 'Left, Right, technocratic and environmentalist desires to condense cities by housing their working classes at battery densities. As fast as the people vote with their feet to lower the densities of the old slums, misguided governments try to rebuild the old densities vertically'. But the tide of suburbia rolls on, and sooner or later the administrators will have to face up to the fact that there is no stopping it. In the 1970s and 1980s there has been a significant rise in the proportion of Australians willing to live in home units, flats, etc.; in 1976, about 20 per cent of all home dwellings were flats and units, compared with only 5.4 per cent in 1954. So the high-density advocates, and of course the sheer advantages of high-density living, are making some headway. But the clear preference of most Australians for a house on its own block of land means that our cities, whether we like it or not, are going to get bigger, and we will all have to come to terms with the way of life that most people prefer.

That means suburbia.

I've defended suburbia so often in the past, from *People, Politics and Pop* onwards, that I don't think it's necessary to go into it all again. The self-contained house on its own block of land seems to me an ideal solution to the problems of family living, even if we choose to live in alternative modes before we have children (commune, tent, caravan, single-person flat) or when we get old (row house, unit, community centre). Most people live in suburbs; I suspect the people who keep knocking suburbia don't like the people who live there either. Behind the bash-suburbia syndrome lurks a real distrust and suspicion of, you know, proles, Norms, ockers, ordinary people, 'the mass' . . .

Up on the north coast of New South Wales there's what used to be a small country town called Alstonville which has expanded dramatically into one of those Gold Coast-type centres of gracious two-storey, three-garage, brick veneer homes set on fenceless expanses of lawn, each one slightly skewed from the next, clustered around contrived cul-de-sacs, and tucked securely away from expressways, pollution, the common world. Awfulville, the local students call it, and I can see why. It's a style taken over from wealthy American ex-urban developments and it has a whiff of class and exclusiveness about it. One architectural critic I know loathes it; he wants people to live in Scandinavian-style courtyard houses, conjoined, in a highly designed blend of togetherness and privacy. In a way it's an upbeat version of the conflict which all Australian cities face: high-density urban or low-density suburban?

Now, I have nothing against courtyard houses. If I could have afforded it, I would have lived in one years ago. Instead, my family and I ended up living in a terrace house, which is a sort of nineteenth-century mass-housing version of the modern courtyard formula except the courtyard is the *back*-yard. But courtyard and town houses tend to be small and cramped, with hardly room for a garage, much less a workshop, and the private outdoor space can be a bit claustrophobic. Whereas the house surrounded by its own land can afford to be spacious, it can expand, it can have a cluster of subsidiary structures (garages, workshops, studio, aviary, chook run, granny flat), it can have its own vegetable garden, and fruit trees, and beehives, it can have a swimming pool, and an all-purpose backyard, and flower gardens, and those lawns which we all like to mow ... I mean, it's significant that almost every architect I know lives in a self-contained house on its own block of land, designed to suit him (or her) self, just as everyone else wants to, and even the critic I mentioned before happens to live in, of all places, a rambling old house set about with trees, gardens, rock walks, and some of the loveliest views to be had on the Palm Beach peninsula! What's good enough for me, apparently, is not what's good enough for everyone else.

To return to Awfulville: in many ways, despite its posh overtones, it represents an image of what most Australians are striving to achieve in their home environment. Space, privacy, and a bit of bush. This last is not to be underestimated; in the last decade or so there has been an enormous change in the attitude of many Australians to the bush, native trees, and the Australian landscape generally, and it isn't just the trendy professionals who want to incorporate that into their living environment. Even the most rapacious developers now realise the value of leaving trees and natural bush on their home sites and the newspapers are full of ads for housing estates placed in the Oz version of a 'sylvan setting'. Look, those houses in Awfulville are really just mini-versions of what, over the centuries, has come to be regarded as one of mankind's most desirable residences: the English stately home. That, too, had its own gardens, lawns, fish ponds, animals, space, the sense of living in a natural yet cultivated context. It, too, had no fences or courtyard walls, but lawns running freely away from the house, set about with shrubs, with a coach (car) driveway curving up to the front door ... sure, here the scale is smaller and the neighbours closer, but the central image and ideal remain the same. And they work. Even those trad cheek-by-jowl suburbs which we are all familiar with, such as La Trobe in Melbourne or Bankstown in Sydney, manage to grab some of the same advantages; sometimes the front yards have almost disappeared, but the backyards ... the *backyards*! They are the focus for the sort of rich popular culture, meaning everything from raising chooks-and-chokos to giving the car a decoke and valve grind to building a boat to having a barbecue to holding a party to, even, just muckin' around with the kids, which makes life worthwhile for a lot of people. Peter Myers, a Sydney architect, argues that Bankstown is a good example of a highly successful, integrated suburb with a 'popular' architecture which allows people to add to or subtract from their houses at will, work in front and backyards, grow their own vegetables and livestock, convert to workshops and cottage industries, and generally create their own subsistence style of living in the very heart of the urban jungle. Try that in your courtyard house! In fact, you can stick it up your town house too ...

The High-Rise
The main disadvantage of the detached house is that it contributes enormously to urban sprawl, and that, I agree, is a problem. It's one of the reasons why so many architects and town planners have turned to that aggro symbol of modern architecture, the high-rise. Because of its economical use of land,

the high-rise was once considered an alternative to urban expansion, but in fact the most it can do is slow down the rate of expansion. Our cities, it seems to me, are going to keep ballooning outwards, no matter how many high-rises are built (Sydney's population is almost static, but the new housing estates keep spreading further and further afield). High-rises provoke extreme reactions in people. In upper-class Darling Point, in Sydney, the high-rises that tower over the harbour foreshore contain the most prestigious and sought-after home units in the city; in working-class Waterloo, the high-rises are often regarded as prisons from which people are desperately trying to escape.

To understand this paradox, we have to understand that *a building is a social construct.* Any building. High-rise, low-rise, stadium, skyscraper, bung. What the building is and how it functions are determined more by social environment than architectural character. And how good a building is depends basically upon how well it responds to the social demands made upon it. Once we perceive this, we can clear a way through a lot of the nonsense which is talked about Australian suburbia, and urban redevelopment, and much else besides.

A high-rise building, for instance, does not exist in a vacuum: it is almost nonsensical to talk about its intrinsic faults and virtues. There are some disparities in design and finish between a tower block in Darling Point and one in Waterloo, but even if the two buildings were physically identical they would be different. And that difference would depend on the social factors which make some high-rises desirable places to live in, and some not.

For one thing, who lives there? People who can afford to look after the building and who like this style of living, or people who are used to ground-level living, gardens, and backyard gossip? Are they poor, handicapped, with lots of kids? Why are they living there? Because they want to, or because they have been virtually forced to, having nowhere else to live?

What is the neighbourhood like—violent? friendly? ugly? What are the local shops and schools like? How close is the high-rise to public transport? How far from the centre of the city or from where most of the inhabitants work? What's the view like? How noisy is the area? How polluted is it?

What is the general response of the people living there to the building? Do they hate it or love it?

You could plonk the glossiest Darling Point skyscraper down in Waterloo, fill it with the destitute, the socially handicapped, the out-of-work, the black, the dislocated and the victims and turn it into a vertical slum within a few months. As (predictably) the crime rate rose, people would be busting to get out. In a way, that's what the New South Wales Housing Commission has done at Waterloo and what other authorities have done elsewhere. It is *exactly* what was done at Pruitt-Igo, the infamous high-rise project in St Louis, U.S.A., where finally the planners and civic leaders gave up and blew the massive complex to pieces with gelignite. There can be few more symbolic images of the modern urban crisis that the sight of the multi-million-dollar, super-mod Pruitt-Igoe skyscrapers, home of thousands of poor black ghetto families, crumbling into dust as explosions ripped the place apart. At least in the U.S. they blow 'em up. In Australia we are left with pathetic, foot-high graffiti letters scrawled across the blank walls: NO MORE WATERLOOS.

There is no such thing, therefore, as architecture in the abstract. The social demands made upon architecture make questions of visual style and finish not irrelevant, but secondary. A successful building is not one which looks stunning in an architectural magazine, or wins a good taste award, but which satisfies the needs and desires of the people who *use* it, who are not necessarily the same as those who *own* it. The users include the more general community who walk past it, see it, live in its shadow, or, more rarely, bask in its reflection. It is a truism that architects are no longer designing buildings; they are involved in creating environments, and as such must bear some of the responsibility for making those environments as we want them to be.

The Urban Crisis

The debate about suburbia is only part of a more general and more crucial debate about the future of our cities. The collapse of the building boom in Australia has done more than leave behind empty office blocks, half-finished spec buildings and vast outer suburban developments bereft of social support sys-

tems. It has highlighted a growing urban crisis which is familiar overseas, but which Australians are just beginning to
confront. At a time of low growth, high unemployment and a
sabotaged social welfare system, it has deepened the conflicts
between Australians and produced a pervasive sense of living
in a pressure cooker. And among architects and town planners it has created a crisis of confidence which takes the form
of: where have we gone wrong?

Because something *has* gone wrong. Australian cities are
now just as bad as (sometimes worse than) their overseas
counterparts. They suffer from pollution, traffic jams, over-
crowding, broken-down services, a frantic competitiveness
and a sense that they no longer reflect the needs of the people
who live in them. There have been attempts at 'development'
and 'redevelopment'; but these, too often, have only made the
situation worse. In fact it is worth looking closely at the reality behind those words to see how the system actually works.

Most development, for a start, is carried out for private
profit by private entrepreneurs who don't give a damn about
community interests. Their only aim is to get the building up
as quickly as possible, with as a high a floor-site ratio as possible, and then sell it, lease it or use it. In the 1960s and 1970s
there emerged the speculative developer who had no idea who
the clients of a building might be or what their needs were,
much less what the needs of the local community might be.
The general idea was to take the money and run. Sometimes
the developer had to conform to a civic building code, but that
was about as far as the civic consciousness of the project went.
Most developments carried out in Australia today are of that
kind; they are private, speculative and aimed at making
money.

'Redevelopment' is of a similar nature except that it is often
undertaken by government housing authorities as part of
their slum clearance and urban renewal programmes. In
theory it is well-intentioned; in practice it is usually carried
out at the expense of working-class communities who have
their houses ripped down over their heads and are then 'relocated', typically, in grim high-rise projects or in outer suburban estates where any sense of community is irretrievably
lost. The process is seen at its worst in the old inner-city sub-

urbs where property values have risen dramatically and the old working-class inhabitants have been moved out and replaced by high-income, high-rent newcomers.

In the last decade, the urban renewal programmes of the United States and similar mass housing projects in Great Britain and Australia have run into fierce opposition from residents, community groups, politicians and trade unionists (e.g., the Builders' Labourers' Federation green bans). Influential critics such as Malcolm MacEwen, author of *Crisis in Architecture*, and Robert Goodman, associate professor of architecture at the Massachusetts Institute of Technology (M.I.T.) and author of *After The Planners*, have attacked the inhumanity and class manipulation of the entire process. And they have singled out for particular criticism the architects, often faceless men in big corporations and housing commissions, who have lent themselves to the worst sort of social engineering. This has spilled over into a general criticism of modern architecture and its lack of responsiveness to the mundane demands and needs of ordinary people. Too many architects, obsessed with the idea of high-density living, have crammed displaced families into totally unsuitable high-rise 'beehives' characterised by high rates of crime, suicide and social distress. Sometimes these architects have been motivated by a genuine desire to help solve the problems of urban sprawl, but their solutions have often been (to paraphrase Hobbes) cheap, nasty and brutish. Writes Bryce Mortlock, partner in one of Australia's leading architectural firms:

> The wind whistles through the undercrofts of the post-Corbusier skyscraper slums ... the spaces between skyscrapers became no man's land, owned and loved by nobody. As to land-use efficiency, the residential densities were no higher than the Georgian squares of London ... Insofar as architecture claimed to change the world, the world has given it the thumbs down.

And MacEwen, who visited Australia in the 1970s, argues in a critique which has been widely reprinted by the Royal Australian Institute of Architects:

> Most of the towers and slabs of the 1960s stand as monuments not to cheapness and efficiency but to waste and extravagance, contriving nevertheless to be sordid and mean,

unsuited to the needs of their inhabitants, dehumanising, and, incidentally, so costly that their rents are far beyond the capacity of poor tenants to pay without subsidies ... The one thing the system cannot produce is low-cost housing.

Another sign of the revolt against the imposed social solutions of modern architecture is the popular criticism that modern glass box skyscrapers are 'inhuman' and 'faceless'. Of course, they are. They are usually secondhand versions of the International style perfected by Mies van der Rohe, the great designer of American corporate skyscrapers, translated to different environments and lacking even the high gloss of their U.S. counterparts. The result is what Patrick McCaughey, professor of visual arts at Monash University, has described as 'unarchitecture'. For Bob Connell, professor of sociology at Macquarie University, they have a clear symbolic significance:

The office towers containing the headquarters of the great companies symbolise to everyone who can see them—and everyone can—their confidence, resources and technological style. Around and among them are developed display windows for consumer capitalism, the networks of glossy arcades that interlace the city centres. The dirt of actual production has mostly been moved out of the city centres into rings of industrial suburbs, so that the bulk of workers now come into their own urban centres only as suppliants (visiting offices) or customers (visiting shops).

What to do about it all?

Some architects, secure in their selfish professionalism, ignore it and hope it will go away. They continue designing individual houses for a select élite, even though they know that the one-off house is an architectural dinosaur; these days less than 3 per cent of houses built are individually designed by an architect. Others, more humanist and aware, move into project homes which at least hold out the hope of mass production of 'good design'. I'm heartened by that, and by the spread of skilfully designed project and kit homes through (usually middle- to upper-class) suburbia; but as architects such as Terry Dorrough (Merchant Builders) and Michael Dysart (Habitat) have found, there are limitations: you don't know the user, you don't know the site, materials have to be cheap to cut costs—and you still only make a small dent in the mass home market.

Some become academics, or consultants, or commentators. They become concerned with the aesthetics of architecture as an art, formal qualities (Venturi v. Kahn), the saving of graceful old buildings and the production of technically skilled but socially illiterate architecture graduates. Their enduring image is that of a tiny man pissing up against the glass curtain wall of an enormous corporate skyscraper; he doesn't notice it is dribbling into his shoe.

Some retreat into mud brick houses (Alistair Knox), solar heating, methane gas energy and the low-cost self-built alternative shelter, hoping that the self-sufficient solution may become the general one. It won't. Constructing an environment through handicraft techniques can be personally satisfying for a very limited number of people, argues Goodman in *After The Planners*, but what is really needed are techniques by which huge numbers of ordinary non-professionals can manipulate their environment for themselves.

At the other end of the scale are the technologists, exponents of concrete solutions to social dilemmas. They tend to admire Bucky Fuller, who thought the earth's energy supply was inexhaustible, and of course Corb (Le Corbusier), who first sketched out those high-rises set in urban desertscapes, and Paolo Soleri, designer of futuristic anthill cities (a cruel joke?). MacEwen provides the best answer:

Brutalist architecture, by definition, is intended as a brutal slap in the face of the public and users. The mere use of the term reveals an extraordinary degree of insensitivity to, and ignorance of, ordinary people, and can be explained only by the isolation of the architect. He is typically a middle-class man, living in the suburbs, keen to escape to the country, and keen, too, on the far more extensive use of plastic, steel and concrete ... The innumerable buildings with drab, grey, begrimed, streaky, cracked concrete finishes, designed with little understanding of drips and weathering or designed to be covered with paint that the client cannot afford, are silent witnesses to the technological inadequacy of the architectural profession ... The use and abuse of concrete, perhaps more than anything else, account for the hostility to many recent buildings and to the architects who are rightly held largely responsible for them. And some architects, God help us, become planners.

Planning has become such a dirty word in the United States and Great Britain, where masses of people have suffered the shock of being ripped out of their homes and relocated in vertical ghettos or satellite oases, that it's almost endearing to find in Australia someone like Hugh Stretton in his recent books advocating a humane, paternalist 'cultural mix' of different groups and classes within planned suburbs. I respond to Stretton's pluralism, the way he cares for people, and his own personal commitment to 'responsive' planning. But it doesn't often work like that. Most of the people who move into planned developments, indeed, who need them most, are the underprivileged groups whose plight is so desperate that any attempt at a restricted social mix becomes inhumane. People need houses badly and planner-bureaucrats have to provide them. Most planning does *not* involve those who are going to live there, though there have been some half-hearted attempts at community participation; and most new housing projects have, *per se*, to be in outer suburban areas which suffer from all the disabilities which even the most careful planning can't avoid. Also, as Stretton admits in *Capitalism, Socialism and the Environment*, 'Forward planning of urban growth becomes a speculators' guide. There has to be reliably puritanical government to keep the system honest at all. Honest or not, bigger and unfairer fortunes are often made in regulated land markets than in open markets'. You don't have to look beyond the Victorian lands scandal, involving deals between the Housing Commission and speculators' agents, and the choosing of quite unsuitable land, to see what goes wrong.

The alternative, urban redevelopment, is highly discriminatory; as I have pointed out, it is usually the poorer, working-class areas which are singled out for destruction and 'renewal'. Middle-class, affluent suburbs are more skilful at organising protests about the bulldozing of their homes for freeways, railways, shopping centres and other redevelopment projects. Paddington, now a wealthy and fashionable Sydney suburb, was able to reject a Department of Main Roads proposal to carve a freeway through its beautiful late-

Victorian terraces, but the same D.M.R. pushed a freeway through the lower-middle- and working-class (and no less beautiful) terraces of Bondi Junction, just a few kilometres away. That entire Eastern Suburbs transport programme is an ironic example of social planning in action. Projections show that there is likely to be little rise in the future population of these well-to-do suburbs, yet they are now served by the first new underground railway to be built in Sydney this century, plus the Eastern Suburbs expressway. The State Labor government hesitated to build the expressway at all, but succumbed to pressure from the commercial developers at Bondi Junction; besides, the D.M.R. had already ripped the houses down. Right now the concrete expressway pylons soar above the terrace houses, carrying traffic and shoppers to one of the fastest-growing commercial centres in Australia. The political nature of expressways can be seen in two linked events: the decision of the New South Wales Labor government to abandon some planned inner-urban expressways in order to save domestic homes, and the junk barriers that the people of Fitzroy put up to try to stop the C7 expressway going through their suburb. (The mayors of Fitzroy and Collingwood had to be arrested and dragged away.) 'I'd like to see them try and put an expressway through Toorak', said one angry resident whose home was being torn down. Writes Robert Goodman, 'We're the soft cops. We're more sophisticated, more educated, more socially conscious than the generals. Planners want "social change"; they deal in words, drawings, programmes and buildings, not guns and napalm'. But, he says, their functions are similar. 'At best we help ameliorate the condition produced by the status quo; at worst we engage in outright destruction.'

In Australia the conflict between planners and people, expressway engineers and resident groups, developers and conservationists, has not yet reached the pitch of intensity it has elsewhere. Where I was living in New York, white cops armed with automatic weapons, tear gas, and Tactical Police Force helmets were evicting black squatters from tenements which Columbia University wanted to tear down for high-rise, high-income tenant development. (It was a similar act by Columbia that sparked off the great student revolts of the late

1960s.) But as Australia's urban problems grow and violence swells and the unfairness of it all becomes more and more apparent, the conflicts will deepen.

Architecture, like art, is a social act. Every building which is raised affects everyone else. Every building that is razed affects everyone else. Nobody has the right, any longer, to build what he wants where he wants it. The 'client' is no longer just the owner, or the developer, or the planner, or the Department of Main Roads, or a government administration. *The client is the community itself.* This means the architect is now in the same position as the politician, or the public servant, or the journalist; he is responsible not just to the boss, the owner, or even a paternalistic Housing Commission, but to the people at large. He is a public figure, publicly accountable.

McEwen spells this out. The first responsibility of architects, he says, is to reduce the consumption of energy and other scarce resources. The second is to make sure that

their skills and the nation's scarce resources are applied to the satisfaction of the essential needs of the community . . . The increase in the size of the public and private corporations, the scale of their operations, and the emergence of the rootless developer to whom building is simply a means of making money, have widened the gap between the architect and the consumer into a gulf. They have also distorted social priorities . . . The profitability of land speculation and development, coupled with the financial constraints of the public authorities, have allowed the poison generated by the property boom to seep right through the profession. It has corrupted small architects as well as big, and forced official architecture into a mould shaped by meanness, artificially high costs, and a bureaucratic approach.

It's easier to point to the problems than the solutions. Ideally, valuable urban land should be taken out of the hands of the speculators and private developers, so that it can be used for community rather than for private interest. In England, the government was forced to take over developable land to prevent the sort of building and property speculation which made London one of Europe's ugliest examples of post-war development. In Canberra a start has been made along these lines, so that the most highly planned of Australia's cities has at least been saved from land speculation; but one can't see pro-development premiers such as Joh Bjelke-Petersen leaping at the idea of nationalising land. One way forward is to accept the reality of suburban expansion and work out ways of dealing with it. This means a complex response, and the investment of a great deal of planning resources and finance. The problems of isolation and high-cost services, to say nothing of the Mount Druitt syndrome of high child population, high unemployment, high deprivation, and high social crime rate, can only be met by a massive investment in public facilities such as community centres, child care centres, social services, transport, parks, schools, sewerage—the whole spectrum of modern support systems. The community is going to need these, whether homes spread out along the ground or up in the air. As inner-urban redevelopments have shown, the need for support systems is just as great there, especially in the high-rise ghettos which have been mistakenly built in the last two decades, as in the outer suburbs. The Liberal-N.C.P. co-alition government in Canberra, ignoring Galbraith's classic analysis of private affluence and public squalor, tried to reduce public expenditure in exactly these areas. At least Whitlam got that one right.

The public housing authorities, for all their dismal record in the past, offer more hope than the private developers. There are signs that they are now prepared to admit to some of the mistakes of the past, and old-style 'slum clearance' schemes have virtually been abandoned. Sub-standard districts should be refurbished, not demolished; in England, for instance, a highly successful scheme for the improvement of existing homes through government subsidy has been in existence for years. Public housing has to become responsive to the needs and demands of the people who are going to live there; that means identifying them, first of all, and then involving them in co-operative schemes and in all stages of design and planning. These same housing authorities are now coming around to the idea of medium-density instead of high-density housing; instead of high-rises they have begun building town houses, terraces, semi-detached cluster housing, and so on. That's a step forward; despite the disadvantages of such housing solutions, they offer a way out of the 'vertical slum' impasse. A mix of low-, medium- and high-density development is probably what we need right now. The best answer to the problem of housing the poor is to have a society in which there are no poor, but until that happens people have to live somewhere, and that means reforming the state authorities so that they create humane, popular, socially constructive environments.

To repeat: a building is a social construct. To change our architecture, and our cities, we have to change the social context. A ghetto or a slum is only a desirable inner-city area in which the 'wrong' people live. There's nothing wrong with the inner city itself; only the social conditions distinguish Aboriginal Redfern from exclusive Woollahra. It's not the architecture, the buildings which made a ghetto something to escape from; it's the conjunction of social forces which destroys the environment and distorts the people who live there. The only real solutions to the urban crisis are political, and to make our cities fit to live in for everyone, we all have to become politicians first and homebodies last.

1981

Politics

10. Hegemony in the Real World

'Hegemony' is one of those words which is so fashionable these days it makes you scared to use it. Yet because it explains so many things about contemporary society—especially Australian society—it's worth persevering with. If you want to understand why Australia seems less likely to have a revolution than any other country in the Western world, or why the Australian people accepted so meekly the dismissal of their elected government by a governor-general in 1975, or why a small élite so easily dominates Australian society, or indeed if you want to understand any of the salient features of Australian politics and social organisation during the last three decades, you have to understand the concept of hegemony.

I first came across the word when I was studying ancient history at school. My history teacher, Harry Nicolson, used it to explain how the most powerful of the Greek city-states, such as Sparta and Athens, exercised control over their neighbours without ruling them *directly*, or conquering them through armed force. The concept went further than mere spheres of influence. Athens, for instance, exerted such dominance over its client states that it virtually ruled them; it was an exercise in—and I still remember him scribbling the word across the blackboard—hegemony.

I next came across the word, as a dominant concept, in the work of the Italian Marxist thinker Antonio Gramsci, and it is basically because of his writing, and of those who have been influenced by him, that the idea has achieved such intellectual currency. Although Gramsci was writing in the 1920s and 1930s, was jailed by Mussolini and died in 1937, it was only in the 1960s and 1970s that his work was translated into English and became freely available, which is the major reason for the time lag between when he wrote and the dissemination of his ideas in English-speaking countries. Another reason is that Gramsci's concept of hegemony seems particularly appropriate to what Kahn and Pepper are pleased to call A.C.Ns, or Advanced Capitalist Nations, and helps explain why these countries, instead of fulfilling Marx's prophecies of revolution, still seem to be firmly in the grip of small ruling élites which exercise power as effectively and sometimes as ruthlessly as ever. It was certainly an Australian ruling élite—Bob Connell, professor of sociology at Macquarie University, calls it a 'ruling class'—which engineered the sacking of Whitlam on 11 November, 1975, the dismissal of the Labor government and the appointment of a conservative government headed by Malcolm Fraser. No warning, no legality, no vote and scarcely a squeak from the Australian populace either. MAINTAIN THE RAGE, said Whitlam. A friend suggests it should have been MAINTAIN THE WHIMPER. What Whitlam came up against was not force, armed force, of the sort which European countries that have experienced fascism and Soviet-style communism are familiar with, but power. You don't have to carry a gun to rule Australia. If you dominate the key institutions, and offices, and media systems, and positions, and hierarchies of control, a stroke of the pen will do.

By hegemony, as I understand it, Gramsci meant the ideological and cultural control which a small ruling group exercises over the rest of society. In *Gramsci's Marxism*, Carl Boggs gives a fuller summary:

> Gramsci meant the permeation through civil society—including a whole range of structures and activities like trade unions, schools, the churches, and the family—of an entire system of values, attitudes, beliefs, morality, etc., that is in one way or another supportive of the established order and the class interests that dominate it. Hegemony in this sense might be defined as an 'organising principle', or world-view (or combination of such world-views), that is dif-

fused by agencies of ideological control and socialisation into every area of daily life. To the extent that this prevailing consciousness is internalised by the broad masses, it becomes part of 'common sense'; as all ruling élites seek to perpetuate their power, wealth and status, they necessarily attempt to popularise their own philosophy, culture, morality, etc., and render them unchallengeable, part of the natural order of things ... From Gramsci's perspective, what was missing [from classical Marxism] was an understanding of the subtle but pervasive forms of ideological control and manipulation that served to perpetuate *all* repressive structures ... Ideological domination rather than direct political coercion had become the primary instrument of bourgeois rule—a generalisation that may help to explain the subtle but effective assimilation of the proletariat in the post-Second-World-War period.

The result: rule of the governors with the consent of the governed.

Of course, part of Gramsci's theory has become the accepted wisdom of our time. The role of the mass media in manipulating the consent of the great majority of people to the rule of a powerful élite by daily bombarding readers and listeners and viewers with a view of the world which supports the established system is now well known. Media news and views, in general, are *against* trade unions, protests, demonstrations, socialism, the Labor Party, 'left-wingers', activists, sexual freedom movements, 'dole bludgers' and strikes; they are *for* free enterprise, employers, profits, development, the churches, private schools, governors, governor-generals, medals, honours, the Liberal Party and free competition (except for themselves). At the time of the 1975 election, every major newspaper, radio station and TV channel in Australia opposed the Labor Party. In all elections the great mass of the media are anti-Labor (the exceptions are famous, and merely prove the rule). Every major Australian media company supported the war in Vietnam. Every single one supported conscription. That in itself ought to give us pause.

What is less evident, perhaps, is the way in which the media present us with a very class-based view of things. In Australia

that view is predominantly middle to upper class. Much of
the news, as survey analysis has shown, is about businessmen,
politicians, academics, professionals, heads of corporations,
institutions and pressure groups; in other words, those who
have succeeded in the system. A great deal of newspaper
space and air time is given over to what they say. It's their
values, attitudes and preoccupations which are reflected
daily, in thousands of ways; so are the values and preoccupations of those who would like to be like them. You rarely hear
about the losers. They're not news. The effect of this is to condition people to assume that some people are intrinsically
more important than others, their attitudes and beliefs are
more valuable than others, and what they do and say is probably right. It's accepted that managers and owners of big corporations should advise the government—for their own
benefit. John Laws spouts the doctrine of the self-made man,
John Singleton proves that crude and rude equals money, Ron
Barassi, football star turned businessman, says you too can
make it if you try. Nobody questions the ethics of a system
which churns out a few winners like these at the cost of making everyone else failures. It's taken for granted that working
people should work hard, companies should make big profits
and that what counts is not the mass of the people but the few
individuals who dominate them. The history of our times, as
presented by the media, is the history of the ruling élite.

The advertising industry, which keeps the media chains
going (not a single newspaper could afford to be published
without ads) reinforces this media barrage. It basically pro-
motes the idea that everything is good as it is. There are exceptions and most advertising campaigns may promote only a
single product or range of products. But the cumulative effect
is one of extolling the way things are. The TV images which
bombard us are of happy, affluent, middle-class families in
happy, affluent, middle-class homes. The going's great, mate.
Buying's good. Loans are good. Development is good. God, the
churches and chambers of commerce are good. The media is
good. THE SYSTEM IS GOOD.

The point is so obvious it scarcely bears restating, yet some
people still resist it and talk sceptically of 'conspiracy theories'. There is no conspiracy; there's no need for one. When I

was a cadet reporter on the *Sydney Morning Herald*, our chief sub-editor, Lewis Townsend, asked our cadet class how newspapers influenced their readers. Why, through their editorials, we chorused. No, replied Townsend, an irascible yet kindly man who knew what the world was about: through their news pages. He was right. Hardly anybody reads the editorials, and only fools believe them. But everybody reads the news (almost). What the media inflict on the Australian public every day is a form of cultural brainwashing, subtle and unsubtle. The first works best, but the second can come in handy too. I'm reminded of what Rupert Murdoch said to Lang Hancock when he wanted to invest in Western Australia's booming mineral discoveries and Sir Charles Court, later premier of the State, seemed reluctant to let Murdoch in. 'Tell Charlie Court,' said Murdoch, 'he can have a headline or a bucket of shit a day.' Now, there's power, *real* power, for you!

The media, however, present us with only one example (and a very familiar one) of the sort of cultural conditioning I'm talking about. If we add to the media the combined weight of most of the key institutions of our society, from schools to churches to the law to the police to the advertising industry to banks, insurance companies and all our major financial institutions, then we begin to get some idea of the phenomenal amount of ideological force which presses in upon us every day of our lives. Social myths and rituals, from Anzac Day to vice-regal ceremonies to the bestowal of medals and honours and titles to the use of paramilitary devices like salutes, sirs and parade-ground drills—in many Australian schools kids still salute the flag and are marched into the classroom!—reinforce the dominance of the established order. (I once received a silver medal from the Queen; I sent it back to her viceroy, John Kerr). The pressure, overtly or subliminally, is always to accept things as they are. Alternatives come to seem utopian, wrong, or impossible; 'pie-in-the-sky'. Gramsci was thrown into prison, became ill after years of confinement, and died shortly after his release; but, if you can construct an ideological prison in everyday society, you don't have to go that far. Instead of jailing socialists, you turn socialism into a dirty word and achieve the same result.

If things don't work out, the full burden of blame is placed upon the individual rather than the system. He's the failure. As Gramsci pointed out, 'all areas of hegemony function together, with varying impact and emphasis from one context to another, to produce and reify a generalised alienation that results in passivity, a sense of powerlessness, sub-cultural fragmentation, separation of the personal and political . . .' (Carl Boggs). *A sense of powerlessness*: it is perhaps the most widespread and insidious social disease of our time, and beautifully suited to those who *do* have power. So is the technique of transferring blame to individuals, e.g., the 'dole bludger' syndrome which operates during times of economic recession. Instead of the system being held responsible for high unemployment, as it should, the people who can't get work are blamed. One result of this is that many of those who don't have jobs begin to accept that it really *is* their fault; out-of-work school leavers lose heart, stop looking for the jobs they can't find, lock themselves in their homes, turn to the telly (or drugs), internalise the system's guilt. They are politically powerless, economically impotent, socially outcast. In England, years of frustration spills over into street riots, and the Liverpool ghettos go up in flames; in Australia the out-of-work are still firmly under control.

After a while, people begin to accept that *how things are* is *how things should be*. To make the conceptual jump outside your own existing social framework is extraordinarily difficult. You may perceive that particular things are wrong, or unfair, or that you personally are being treated badly; but to jump outside the entire commercial system in which you grew up, to reject the total organisation of society, let alone imagine a realistic alternative—that seems impossible. The weight of *how things are* is almost irresistible. I remember riding on the top floor of the double-decker bus from Haberfield to Cranbrook school each morning, watching the grimy industrial suburbs and galvanised iron awnings-tops and rubbish-littered footpaths reel backwards through my mind, watching the people in overcoats and felt hats and florals waiting for bus 459 and bus 461 on street corners in Annandale, Leichhardt, Petersham, Pyrmont, Surry Hills, and noticing the American cars slide by, as Lowell says, with a 'savage servility', and knew it was all both ugly and wrong; but, hour after hour, watching darkness turn the suburbia of Sydney's inner west into fragile glass, I still couldn't quite work out how it could be any different. Or what the difference would look and feel like. Go to sleep. Pull your felt hat down over your eyes. Sometimes I woke up in Concord. Going through it the other day, row after row of neat brick bungalows with neat front lawns, I wondered whether everyone there was still asleep.

The most insidious aspect of this form of social and cultural control is its subterranean quality, the fact that it exists with our hardly being aware of it. You grow up in Australia and take it for granted that you'll go to work for a company which is owned by someone else, that you may spend your life working for the same boss but that you'll never *be* the boss. A few Australians might have heard of the idea of the workers owning and controlling their own factories, or companies, or industries, but hardly any of them believe it is really possible. Thousands of Australians every day catch the ferry to Circular Quay in Sydney, but, as they stare at the corporate skyscrapers lining the waterfront few of them question whether those corporations have any right to that massive concentration of wealth and power, or whether they shouldn't perhaps be government or community blocks, responsible to and owned by the people. In Mitterrand's France, 40 per cent of industry is state-owned, and still more is to be nationalised; in Australia nationalisation barely comes up for discussion, and a Liberal-Country Party government busily sells off some of the few enterprises the state does run. In Sweden, the manufacture of Volvos is decentralised throughout the countryside so that workers can stay in their own villages and still make cars; at Fishermen's Bend hordes of migrant workers are bussed into an appalling industrial complex to labour on mass production lines. Australians are the heaviest insurers in the world, with bitter memories of the Depression behind them, but as they walk up to the glossy counters of the A.M.P., M.L.C., Sentry, Prudential and so on, few of them realise that these same insurance companies blocked a government scheme to set up a national, community-owned insurance company. Here, the private holds sway. It's simply taken for granted. Private wealth, private land, private monopoly of power ... you rarely hear any argument against it. Private banks? Private schools? Private health funds? Private corporations? Company towns? Private mines? Private police forces? Private planes? Private profit, private development, private everything (including private enterprise)—how could it be any other way?

Until you go overseas, it's hard to believe there *is* any other way. Most Australians never go overseas. They stay at home and get what little information they obtain about foreign countries through the private media. The A.B.C., starved of funds and self-censored, is hardly an alternative. People laugh at Barry Humphries' parodies of the Ugly Aussie, little realising that he's ugly because he doesn't know any better and that Humphries, a bitter political reactionary, is laughing at *them*. At school, Australians aren't taught the basics of their own social system; that might be subversive. In Queensland, you have to get permission from the authorities to protest against the authorities. Everywhere you turn, the subtle network of Orwellian control remains.

The process of acculturation which the system imposes upon its members, and which conditions and manipulates their responses, can be seen in the most trivial and everyday details; even, for instance, in the way certain words are used, and eventually are imbued with a clear political colouration. In Australia, in the media, words such as *left-wing, radical, strike, protest, the unions, feminist,* and *shop steward* are almost always used critically. They are typically used in conjunction with other words which make the weight of contempt and disapproval even clearer, as in *extreme* left-wing, *illegal* strike (whatever that is), *ultra*-feminist. Anyone who grows up in a country in which these ideas and values, and the words which describe them, are perpetually denigrated is bound to be conditioned by that cultural assault.

Take a single word, *strike.* When was the last time any media outlet in Australia approved of a strike? The idea is almost laughable. The strike is one of the great targets of the media, and strikes are virtually always presented unfavourably. They are described as wildcat, illegal, selfish, bloody-minded, a great inconvenience to the public, and above all 'unnecessary'. If you believed the media, strikes should *never* occur; there's no need for them; and, after decades of conditioning, a large section of the Australian (voting) public probably believes the same thing. The public has never had explained to them that strikes are, for a start, an inevitable symptom of the conflict of interests which occurs in any society and is virtually built into the idea of democracy. Nor are they told that going on strike is one of the few ways, and often the only way, in which a working man can influence the politics of his country or his own destiny. The media never explain that the right to refuse to work, to withdraw one's labour, is the only thing that distinguishes the worker from the slave. And certainly they never argue that most strikes are justified (as they are) because they are virtually the only way in which the great mass of people who work for a living can improve their wages and conditions. No: strikes are bad. They're not necessary. After a while union-bashing becomes a profitable sport for Liberal Party politicians, the media cheer from the sidelines, strikes are deliberately provoked just before elections to help damage the Labor Party, and the great Australian public votes 'freely' to perpetuate the control of those who, unbeknown to the voters, already control them.

That's just one word. The exercise could be repeated indefinitely.

Sometimes, as I've said, the control is not so subtle. Police, prisons, security forces, the arbitration system and the courts systematically enforce the existing arrangements. They have other functions too, but basically they uphold the existing system. Hence, to borrow an infamous phrase, 'law and order'. Most Australians accept 'the law' as fair and just; it takes a while to realise that the law fundamentally exists not only to prohibit and settle conflicts but also, socially, to keep things *as they are*, to legalise and legitimise all existing power arrangements. It has little or no interest in change. It takes even longer to realise that some judges and some courts, including the High Court, are biased, reactionary, and, as Sir Garfield Barwick's intervention in the events of 1975 showed, politically corrupt.

Barwick's role in the dismissal of the Labor government is a notorious demonstration of Gramsci's theories. It wasn't necessary, as in Chile, to bomb parliament and execute the elected prime minister. Instead, a former Liberal Party politician used the full weight of his position as chief justice to advise Kerr, wrongly, that he had the power to sack Whitlam; invented the doctrine of the 'caretaker government' so that Fraser could be 'appointed' prime minister; and acted out a nakedly political role of the sort that the constitution express-ly forbids, by giving any advice at all. Kerr used Barwick's legal backing to justify his dismissal of the government. And so two unimpeachably conservative (and powerful) civil posi-tions, that of the chief justice and the governor-general, were used by even more conservative political forces to corrupt and overthrow the democratic process. In Gramsci's view, such civil institutions as the law, education, the media, mass culture, etc., take on a new role in advanced capitalist socie-ties; they become the main agents of class domination, replac-ing the use or threat of physical force. He should have been around in 1975, as the champagne bottles were broken open in the stock exchanges, parliament vainly passed a vote of confi-dence in its Labor prime minister, and the media placards shouted gleefully KERR SACKS WHITLAM.

Gramsci viewed all popular expressions of anger, despair and alienation—of which, one could argue, social criminality is a crucial example—as having the potential to chip away at this form of control; but hanging judges, severe penalties and make-an-example-of-you verdicts reassert the power of the law. Law reformers and law reform commissions can make the law more humane or more efficient, but they don't change its essential hegemonic function. There is something pathetic about the anger of bikies, and punks, and street kids, and most of those scribblers of graffiti on lavatory walls; the other side has all the (real and surrogate) guns.

No wonder, then, that Australia seems so conservative. Many of the potential agents of resistance have been bought or frightened off. There is an immediate outcry if any union involves itself in a 'political' strike or the rank and file take matters into their own hands. The media are more heavily monopolised than anywhere else in the Western world. The education systems of the various states are notoriously rigid and reactionary; tertiary institutions such as universities and colleges are under sustained attack to make them harder to get into, more expensive and more conformist. And, at an everyday level, Australians are subject to a diffuse indoctrination into accepting the system as it is. As I have argued before, this is not absolutely successful; it is sometimes vigorously opposed. But the pressure simply to embrace the status quo is immense.

The trouble with this sort of analysis, of course, is that it can seem so extreme as to be unbelievable. Mere political doctrinalism. I've always been suspicious of such stuff, even of words like 'capitalism'; they seem to be overloaded with too great a weight of ideological bias and cliché. Also, a great deal of the social conditioning I am talking about is unconscious; people in positions of influence and power often project their stances just like anyone else, and might (correctly) resist the idea that what they do is manipulative. Anyhow, they argue, surely things can't be as bad as *that*. And I agree that, in Australia, most people lead lives that are comparatively free and easy; they feel far less oppressed, and are right to do so, than their equivalents in, say, most east European countries. But that's hardly a cause for self-congratulation. It simply means that they have escaped the excesses of state totalitarianism by accepting a much more subtle (and gentler) form of social control. They have, in the main, accepted the limits imposed upon them; they accept the injustices and inequalities of their lives as inevitable; and they have come to think of what happens as natural. That's not an ideological statement; it just is the way things are.

In a way, George Orwell understood it all long ago. I've always thought him a brilliant essayist, and rereading his essay on boys' weeklies made me realise what a perceptive analyst of popular culture he was, long before such analysis had become a standard technique of Left sociology. Writing about what boys wanted from comic books on 'Martians, death-rays, grizzly bears and gangsters' (shades of *Star Wars*!), he says:

> They get what they are looking for, but they get it wrapped up in the illusions which their future employers think suitable for them ... Personally I believe that most people are influenced far more than they would care to admit by novels, serial stories, films and so forth, and that from this point of view the worst books are often the most important, because they are usually the ones that are read earliest in

life . . . Here is the stuff that is read somewhere between the ages of twelve and eighteen by a very large proportion, perhaps an actual majority, of English boys, including many who will never read anything else except newspapers; and along with it they are absorbing a set of beliefs which would be regarded as hopelessly out of date in the Central Office of the Conservative Party. All the better because it is being done indirectly, there is being pumped into them the conviction that the major problems of our time do not exist, that there is nothing wrong with laissez-faire capitalism, that foreigners are unimportant comics . . .

It all sounds dreadfully familiar; and Orwell was writing pre-TV! Towards the end he spells it out even more clearly:

All fiction from the novels in the mushroom libraries downwards is censored in the interests of the ruling class. And boys' fiction above all . . . is sodden in the worst illusions of 1910. The fact is only unimportant if one believes that what is read in childhood leaves no impression behind. Lord Camrose and his colleagues evidently believe nothing of the kind, and, after all, Lord Camrose ought to know.

I doubt if Orwell had ever read Gramsci, or even heard of him, but his approach is remarkably similar. Both men shared a profound suspicion of power élites of any kind, which Orwell was to dramatise in later fiction such as *Animal Farm* and *1984*. Gramsci, on his side, believed that in the long run it was the mass of the people, not merely an organised party leadership, which had to create socialism; the main political task of a socialist movement was to create a 'counter-hegemony' which would break the ideological bond between the rulers and the ruled, and unless socialism was 'organic', a mass movement, it would degenerate into an ideology used by a new élite to consolidate its own power. In *Prison Notebooks*, he wrote:

The same distinction can be made between the notion of intellectual *élites* separated from the masses, and that of intellectuals who are conscious of being linked organically to a national-popular mass. In reality, one has to struggle against the above-mentioned degenerations, the false heroisms and pseudo-aristocracies, and stimulate the formation of homogeneous, compact social blocs, which will give birth to their own intellectuals, their own commandos, their own vanguard—who in turn will react upon those blocs in order to develop them, and not merely so as to perpetuate their gypsy domination.

This is immediately recognisable as a very modern view, and one close to the position worked out by the New Left in Britain and elsewhere. It is little wonder that Gramsci's ideas have been taken up so avidly by a European Left which is conscious on the one hand, of the distortions of Marxism in the Soviet Union and on the other of the failure of revolutions to take place in the advanced capitalist nations of the West. Gramsci's explanation of this second fact was the lack of any mass socialist consciousness which could crystallise the opposition to capitalism, and the failure of the socialist movement to create a counter-hegemonic world view. 'Gramsci insisted that socialist revolution should be conceived of as an organic *process*, not an event (or series of events), and that *consciousness transformation* is an inseparable part of structural change, indeed, that it is impossible to conceptualise them as distinct phenomena' (Boggs). As one of the earliest theoretical critics of advanced capitalism, he has had a profound effect upon later thinkers such as Althusser, Miliband, and the Frankfurt School, including Marcuse.

I haven't even begun to deal, in this too-brief summary, with Gramsci's other theories: his rejection of a purely 'economist' view of culture, his development of the theory of praxis, and his belief that political struggle could not be regarded as a 'pure' manifestation of class conflict but as a process mediated by various issues, priorities, movements and ideological fractions—hence the importance, in my view, of particular movements such as the women's movement, black power and the sexual liberation groups. Gramsci wrote, voluminously, for most of his life; the great bulk of his work is still not readily available. What is important, however, is that its central concepts provide a theoretical framework for understanding the exercise of power in places like Australia—and techniques for changing it.

When I was still a lowly fifth former at school I once asked one of the seniors, a brilliant but somewhat taciturn student who was later to become deputy head of a key Commonwealth department, why he was one of the school's few Labor Party supporters. (Needless to say, private schools are not exactly hotbeds of radical intellectuals.) 'Because,' he replied, after pondering the question at some length, 'socialism is good'. But why, I persisted, was socialism good? This provoked an even longer and more considered silence. 'Because,' he said finally, 'capitalism is bad'. The formidable logic of this approach has never quite deserted me. I have never had any utopian belief that socialism, or a socialist state, would solve the entire spectrum of problems facing twentieth-century technocratic nations/states; the difficulties facing any attempt to make democracy work democratically, to abolish the boss-worker symbiosis (expounded and satirised in Bertolucci's *1900*), and to create genuine equality in our society, are far too intractable for that. Nor have I ever thought, rightly or wrongly, that capitalism alone is the source of the evils of modern society, from war to personal greed to criminality, or that its abolition will create the millennium on earth. I don't believe there is a historical inevitability about the destruction of capitalism, except insofar that all social systems are eventually superseded (capitalism has shown itself to be remarkably resilient so far), nor that one particular class is destined to create 'the revolution'—a piece of Marxist doctrine that seems singularly inappropriate to Australia, where the subdivision and fractionalising of the working class has proceeded with extreme rapidity in the last two decades. It's interesting to me that, as Boggs puts it, Gramsci 'rejected as metaphysics the assumption that particular classes and groups are the historical carriers of a singular revolutionary consciousness, since it ignored the crucial variations of mediating factors *within* classes and from country to country' and that he recognised the importance of 'the tendency towards diversification of the proletariat in advanced capitalism'.

The thesis for the fragmentation of the self-styled middle and working classes in Australia is one I have argued in detail in *The Australian People*. However, it seems clear to me that any system, like our own, which has *at its very core* inequality, competition, profit, private ownership, and the concentration of power into private hands, must be changed. Radically. Ultimately, it must be replaced. Injustice is built into the very structure of the current system; it can be reformed, but reforms which were in any way satisfactory would change its nature utterly. People are too precious, and their lives too short, to have to exist under a form of social organisation which brings out the very worst in humanity—greed, dog-eat-dog competitiveness, the pursuit of private gain at the expense of the common good—and suppresses the best. What we need is an alternative, a system based upon the ideas of co-operation, sharing, and equality. The attempt to construct such an alternative, whether in a bush commune or a Woodstock festival or a political system, is one of the key themes of twentieth-century history.

Though I have had to skate over some of his basic concepts, during his lifetime Gramsci developed very clear strategies for countering the hegemony of the ruling group. They involved, for a start, the penetration and gradual destruction of the dominant belief system; the creation of an alternative system of ideas and values which would embody socialist principles; and a prolonged ideological and cultural struggle to initiate a new 'integrated culture'—indeed, thirty years before the Chinese experience was to make the phrase familiar, Gramsci was advocating a continuing cultural revolution. In other essays in this book I've tried to point out some of the ways in which this process of cultural re-creation might begin; the media are obvious starting points. The *process* of resistance and opposition is important in its own right; virtually every co-operative, commune, dissent movement, resident action group, protest, demonstration, strike, freedom group, act of sharing or exercise of democratic rights is a move in the right direction. A very few of these techniques (e.g., the demonstration) may be used by conservative groups, but in contemporary society most of the opposition comes from those who, at whatever level of awareness, are trying to resist the system which is imposed upon them. Gramsci argued for the creation of durable 'blocs' and popular alliances which, though they may crystallise around particular issues, could be generally radicalising and counter-hegemonic. As someone who marched from Aldermaston to London in the early days, and saw Trafalgar Square fill up with a quarter of a million demonstrators as Bertrand Russell shouted and whispered into the wind, and later witnessed an alliance of radicals, students, blacks, hippies and anti-Vietnam protesters (marching under the original C.N.D. peace symbol) destroy an American president, that makes sense. The ban-the-bomb and anti-Vietnam movements radicalised generations of young people; another issue, or series of conflicts, may perform the same function for a future generation. Despite the traditional emphasis of Marxism upon the economic basis of the ruling culture, and the economic wellsprings of revolution, Gramsci rejected the notion that economics *determined* completely what happened and developed the idea of a cultural/ideological superstructure ... a view which Ian Turner came around to before his death. 'It may be ruled out,' Gramsci wrote in *Prison Notebooks*, 'that immediate economic crises of themselves produce fundamental historical events; they can simply create a terrain more favourable to the dissemination of certain modes of thought, and certain ways of posing and resolving questions involving the entire subsequent development of national life.'

Gramsci's ideas are not to be, and have not been, accepted uncritically. His more orthodox Marxist beliefs are open to the traditional objections of democrats and pluralists; at one stage, unbelievably, he and Mussolini were on the same ideological side—a paradox which George Orwell, for one, would not have found so paradoxical. Indeed, it is his theory of hegemony, which at the time seemed a radical departure from strict Marxist theory, rather than his other concepts which have had such an influence upon contemporary thought. Apart from the sheer persuasiveness of the theory, this may be due in a minor way to the clear function it assigns to intellectuals. 'Every revolution has been preceded by an intense labour of social criticism, of cultural penetration and diffusion,' he wrote. In this labour, he reasoned, intellectuals had a crucial role to play, for the intellectuals were first able to comprehend the intricate workings of the hegemonic state and, comprehending, combat it.

That seems as good a place as any to leave this argument. Gramsci, like Mississippi Fred McDowell, is dead, but his ideas (music) live on. Perhaps it's worth quoting one last extract from the work which, a sick and dying man, he wrote in an Italian prison:

Creating a new culture does not only mean one's own indi-

vidual 'original' discoveries. It also, and most particularly, means the diffusion in a critical form of truths already discovered, their 'socialisation', as it were ... The mode of being of the new intellectual can no longer consist in eloquence, which is an exterior and momentary mover of feelings and passions, but in active participation in practical life, as constructor, organiser, permanent persuader ...
Write on.

1983

11. On Equality

When I was a kid, I always used to be mystified by those tales where the fisherman's wife or whoever it was would be given three wishes by the Good Fairy and they always wished for crazy, self-indulgent things like 'I wish everything I touched turned to gold', and of course it always rebounded on them; I mean, who can eat gold toast? And I always wondered why they didn't wish for something more general, like wishing that everyone in the world (including themselves) should be happy ever afterwards, because then nothing could ever go wrong again and the world would be a perfect place to live in and there wouldn't even be a need for a Good Fairy to dispense dubious favours to favourites; all it needed of the fishermen and fishermen's wives and shoemakers and others was a bit of imagination, and a bit of common sense, and just a hint of generosity . . .

Ah! The birth of utopianism.

Socialism isn't utopian, because no socialist in his (or her) right mind really believes the human race will ever achieve the millennium, or whatever it's called, least of all in our own lifetime—most socialists I know are idealists condemned by the world to be pragmatists—but socialism does hold out the idea of a better life (for everyone) and a better world than the one we currently endure, and has some thought of how we might edge cautiously sideways, like a crab, towards it; and I still think that all that's needed to bring us closer is a bit of imagination, and a bit of common sense, and just a hint of generosity.

Of course, there are always corrupt and siren voices who tell us that human nature can't be changed, that it's dog-eat-dog, every-man-for-himself, you gotta keep ahead of the Joneses, anyone can make it, some are more equal than others, what will be will be, and all the rest of that puerile John Laws shit—it's usually purveyed by pundits, commentators and other Talking Heads on TV, you can pick 'em by their distinguished grey hair and little piggy snouts—but I don't believe a bit of it and I don't think a lot of other people do, either, despite generations of media manipulation and the sort of cultural reinforcement of existing exploitative arrangements which Gramsci talks of, i.e., the terrible dead-and-alive weight of institutions, power groups, class interests, and what my old headmaster used to jovially call 'the haves'; otherwise it would be hard to see why half the Australian people regularly vote Labor and why a great deal of our intellectual and political debate is about what sorts of changes we should make in Australian society and how we should make them, and why, indeed, there would be a socialist movement at all. But there *is* a socialist movement, which is as diverse and argumentative as you would expect any movement to be which cares about freedom, real freedom, such as freedom from want, from fear, from exploitation, and from the life sentence of living powerless in an unjust and unequal society; and it's that movement, with its spin-offs and moral demands and associated ideas and philosophies and initiatives which holds out the best hope for a good life for most people, including most Australians, today.

Despite its theoretical complexity, it seems to me that socialism is based upon some very simple ideas. Like equality. For myself, I think all inequality is wrong. Everyone should be equal, *really* equal: any other way of organising society is manifestly unfair to those (women, blacks, workers, the sick, handicapped, weak, powerless, in fact the majority of people) who suffer so that a small and privileged élite should gain disproportionate power, wealth and the good things of life. This doesn't mean that people are born equal, or the same; obviously they're not. But it means they should *be* equals in the society in which they share and to which they contribute. They should have equal rights, equality before the law and the state, and equal access to education, power, freedom and what Manning Clark calls 'fulfilment'. And that doesn't mean that they should simply have equal opportunities for these things, and then be forced to accept the lottery-of-life results by which there are a few lucky winners and the rest spend their lives in a form of industrial slavery . . . which is basically what happens at present. If you think this is an exaggeration, talk to some of the out-of-work kids who, despite the Fraser government's persecution of 'dole bludgers' and its attempt to stop welfare payments to young people leaving school, refuse to work in a factory. They've been there, or their mothers and fathers have, and they know it for what it is: a charnel house where people live and die in chains. People need equal *rewards*, or at least should be rewarded according to their needs—an old, old principle, so old and honourable that you'd hardly think it needed restating, except that so many politicians spend their time running away from it. I don't believe in a meritocracy, or in grossly unequal rewards being dealt out to people because of merit, luck, effort, the Hand of God, accident of birth, or random arrangement of genes. People have the right to be equal because they are human, and deserve an equal chance at happiness; equality doesn't guarantee happiness, but it increases the chances remarkably (ask any freed slave, or Vietnamese refugee, or political prisoner).

We live in Australia in a society so prosperous overall, so wealthy, so endowed with resources, that the gross and shocking inequalities which we confront every day of our lives are unforgivable, let alone the grander inequality of our position in a world where the great majority of mankind is starving, ill, or poverty-stricken. And yet Murdoch and his hired pens, cartoonists, columnists and editorialists cook up a phony Tax Revolt because, they whine, we don't have enough to spend on ourselves! Unbelievable. Look: I think *everyone should have the same income*, with perhaps adjustments for size of family, disabilities, illness, etc. I can't see any reason to organise it any other way. Nor do I believe any of that stuff about people needing the incentive of greed to work, or compete, or put their best efforts into something. Women and men become nurses, or doctors, or artists, or farmers, or mechanics, or politicians, because they want to, not because of the money; there are a lot of incentives, such as prestige, and job satisfaction, and challenge, and expression of personal skill and ability which, to pitch the argument at its lowest level, can take the place of income incentive; in many occupations they already do. The idea that people need grossly unequal rewards to inspire them to work is a piece of capitalist mythology, perpetuated by those who are already the beneficiaries of massive inequality and who believe that society should be run on a basis of competition instead of co-operation. After all, it's got them where they are.

When I was a secondary modern teacher in England, teaching in a punishment-centred Catholic school in inner London, there was a fiery, rotund, white-haired Welsh teacher (I think he taught maths), in his sixties at least, who used to stand around cheerily drinking coffee and listening to his mates grizzle about school and the government and the Labour Party most of the time; but occasionally, just occasionally, he would lose his temper with all of them and stomp around the room shouting lines from Aneurin Bevan and Keir Hardie and roaring about the social nature of man and ordaining that the highest honour we could have was to work for each other, for the common good; and though, as an ex-student of John Anderson, I am aware of the philosophic problems with the idea of 'the common good' (though not the common *goods*) my heart went out to the man—he was right, and I wish we had some people like him around now, giants, people with Bevan's fire in the belly (an old cliché, but a lovely one) and glory in their heads and some sense that, as Bruce Petty put it in another context, all present arrangements are artificial. Instead of which, back here in Australia, we waddle around in cotton wool with mortgages coiled around our necks and media poison in our ears and, as I said in *The Australian People*, a spike driven by the industrial society right through the heart. And one of these days, I hope, though I believe the crawl sideways is inevitably slow, we will all come to realise what a freaky society this is, how selfish, how far removed from the ideals and high-courage determinations of the rest of the world we are.

And take the ice cream out of our mouths.

Equality! It's a word to make a man bleed. Or make his heart leap. I remember when I was at Cranbrook school, and I was arguing the case for sharing everything around equally, one of my co-pupils asked: 'If *you* had a million pounds, would you give it away?' 'No,' I answered honestly. There was a howl of glee from the other kids standing around (my co-boarders at the time included Charles Lloyd Jones, Kerry Packer, Clyde Packer and others of that ilk): PROOF, they chortled, that the human race was and always would be inordinately selfish. But, as I tried to point out at the time, what the hell was the use of one man giving away a million pounds? *Everybody* had to give something away, everybody who was wealthier than anyone else anyhow; those who were wealthiest gave away most, those who were least wealthy gave away least. (The same principle is enshrined, in mutilated form, in our contemporary system of progressive taxation, though the Queensland flat-rate taxers want to get rid of even that; are they flat-earthers too?) And those who were poorest, and sickest, and least privileged, and had the most human beings to look after, received what the others gave away.

Nobody listened. They walked away.

In Australia we have had a multi-million-dollar tax avoidance business which included illegal 'bottom-of-the-harbour' schemes involving criminals, a High Court which until recently has sanctioned and upheld the most blatant tax avoidance schemes, senior Liberal ministers who have used family trusts and other lurks to avoid paying tax, doctors and Q.C.s who are daily dreaming up new ways of hoarding and holding onto their incredible wealth, mining and oil companies which benefit from extraordinary tax concessions and send much of their profits to parent transnational companies overseas, and a situation in which the poorest 20 per cent of Australians own less than 1 per cent of their country's wealth, while the top 1 per cent of Australians own over 9 per cent of the nation's wealth. They remind me of the kids, with their striped old-school ties, who turned and walked away. One of these days they won't be allowed to walk away.

I've also never understood why we don't make sure that everybody *starts off* equal. I mean, that would be a first step. It would be an obvious way of at least diminishing the inequality which surrounds us. A system like the current one, in which a small minority inherits gross and accumulated amounts of money while the great majority of ordinary people set off to battle their way through life with the chance of even owning a home of their own becoming more and more remote, seems absolutely ludicrous. As the old socialist argument points out, those personal and family fortunes accumulated by the Gettys, Rockefellers, Lloyd Joneses, Baillieus and Knoxes of this world have been created, basically, by the effort, work and resources of the *community*, by the toil of hundreds of thousands of people who work in factories and mines and shops to create that wealth; it should go back to the community, not be hoarded by wealthy families to be passed down from favoured son to favoured son, generation after generation. I personally don't think those fortunes should be allowed to be passed on; they should be appropriated by the community and spent on creating real equality for the next generation of Australians. Hence death duties, which is an unfortunate name for a perfectly valid and fair process. In fact, I'm not really in favour of people inheriting wealth at all; inheritance obviously makes everybody unequal from the start, and makes it even harder to achieve true equality in our society. Of course, everybody likes to pass something on to their children: personal possessions, sentimental things, the family piano, maybe the family home. That seems O.K. to me—as long as everybody has a home to pass on, or a home to live in, or true equality with everyone else in their living conditions. But beyond that, no. No inheritance. Bjelke-Petersen is trying to push us the other way; he's abolished death duties in Queensland, because that favours his rich backers and supporters. People in other states as well have been conned into believing that death duties are somehow immoral, or bad for them, or an attack on their precious individual savings; whereas the attempt to reduce private fortunes, and to have community-created wealth returned to the community instead of being passed on, selfishly, to private individuals, is a highly moral endeavour and something we should all support. No inheritances.

What else?

Well, we have to get rid of those gross and traditional inequalities which confront us every day. Between men and women, for a start. This would require a book (or more) in itself, and not being a woman I am not in the best position to write it; but the formal and informal discrimination which still exists against women, and the inequality of male and female roles, should not be tolerated in any society which is concerned about fairness. Nor should we tolerate the inequalities which still exist among races, among religious groups, between migrants and native-born, among so many other privileged and underprivileged groups in Australia. Religious and racial bigotry isn't nearly as bad now as when I was growing up and learning a whole lexicon of prejudice—wops, dagos, ities, ikeys, rockchoppers, chinks, chows, boongs, abos, niggers, frogs, reffos—but, to take three different examples, Jews, Roman Catholics and Aborigines are still targets of discrimination.

We should not accept inequalities of education: the private schools are the chief sources of this, and in Australia they occupy a position as citadels of power and inherited advantage which is even more marked than in England, whence they came. They should be abolished, or transformed into state schools. I reckon Melbourne Grammar would make a first-class individual school, with its own character and freedom to experiment, within the state system. Easy. I don't want my kids to have special advantages over anybody else's and I don't want anybody else's to have special advantages, either, unless they're handicapped and need help; the only way to ensure that is to have a schooling system as fair, though diverse, as it's possible to devise. Nor does bringing all private schools within the state system mean that schools would become depressingly uniform. There is plenty of variety within the state systems of, for example, England, and the United States, and to a certain extent Australia, and further variety and nonconformity could easily be built in. When I was at Cranbrook I was fortunate to come into contact with some of the best teachers I've ever met: Harry Nicolson, an Andersonian, who had a great influence on me and who became a good friend; C. A. Bell, who taught us English honours; and Mark Bishop, the current headmaster. Manning Clark, bless 'im, taught at Melbourne Grammar! But why should such teachers be available only to those who can afford to send their kids to expensive private schools? I mean, the idea of being able to *buy* your way into special schools, so your kids get special advantages over everybody else in the society, even though they don't deserve it, and of the government (of the people, by the people, for the people) giving immense amounts of money to these schools to fortify their special and unfair place in the community . . . crazy, isn't it? I can't believe it goes on.

Equality of power is something much harder to achieve. Some form of participatory democracy is about as close to achieving it as humanity is likely to come, in governmental terms anyhow; but it would have to be a participatory democracy very different to the travesty of one which exists in Australia right now, where every three years a slightly different segment of the ruling élite presents itself for re-election under a heavily biased electoral system—and then goes ahead and rules as it wishes, with a tame-dog media system in full hue and cry in support of it. A genuinely participatory system of government is one which enfranchises all people so that they are involved in the political process (in its broadest sense) most of the time. Evolving such a system is a much more difficult task in complex modern societies of millions of people than it was in the days of the small Greek city-state, but it is one that, with the aid of contemporary media technology, should not be beyond us. The Greek polity had grievous flaws, just as ours does, but if we wanted to make democratic principles work, I'm sure we could. In other essays in this book I grapple with some ideas about how, culturally at least, this could be done.

Politically? Well, it means reforming and revitalising parliament, for a start; making major changes to the constitution, which Donald Horne, Gareth Evans and others have already canvassed in full; extending the democratic process to the most minor level; and reversing the centralisation of government power, which has steadily developed over the last decades, into the hands of an elected monarch called the Prime Minister. The day after Harold Holt, an affable and consensus-minded man, took over from the Great God Menzies, I went to interview him in the Prime Minister's office and found him standing, very pleased with himself (as well he might be) behind the enormous P.M.'s desk. Dutifully seeking a bit of newspaper 'colour', I asked him what the desk was made of. 'I've no idea, Craig,' he replied, grinning. 'It's the fact that I'm behind it which counts!' Poor Harold. I liked him; he introduced me to the avocado. A streak of good old Aussie hedonism killed him. But even Harold developed a taste for the abuse of power, and proclaimed, sycophantly, 'We are all the way with LBJ' (David Moore took a classic photo of him on that very occasion, head bowed as if in worship, lurking on the dais behind the most powerful Texan in the world)—and sent off conscripts, your sons and mine, to a lottery death in Vietnam. No more Harolds, please.

Giving everyone access to power in the workplace is just as important. Here again, some of the techniques have already been established: self-management, worker control, union ownership, co-operatives, nationalisation. Most of them simply haven't been tried, not with the sort of effort that would be needed to make them succeed—not here, anyhow, though some Scandinavian countries are well down that road. In Australia we are burdened with a ludicrous constitution which, at present, prevents the government nationalising any single industry, though it allows private companies to nationalise any industry they wish simply by setting up a monopoly. Thus B.H.P. has effectively nationalised the steel industry, and C.S.R. the sugar industry, and A.C.I. the glass industry (all monopolies) on behalf of private shareholders. Australia, in fact, is the most highly monopolised and oligopolised nation in the world. But the government, representing the community, is outlawed from touching a single new industry, though it already runs (successfully) most of our vital service industries: water, power, telephones, public transport, the post office, the business of government itself. Actually, the constitution, for all its faults and outdatedness, doesn't really stop the Australian people from owning their own industries and undertakings. A wrong and politically motivated decision by a particular High Court thirty-two years ago, aided by a notorious barrister-politician, Sir Garfield Barwick, who was later to take a hand, illegally, in the dismissal of an elected government, effectively stopped government nationalisation in Australia. In an exercise of nakedly biased power which was to be overshadowed only by the events of 1975, the High Court decided to use the pretext of Section 92 of the constitution, which bars any hindrance to 'interstate trade', to prohibit the nationalisation of any further enterprises—on the grounds that this would restrict trade! In the future, no doubt, a more liberal High Court will reinterpret Section 92 to allow Australians to do what they vote to do; some recent decisions have already started the process, but the damage in the meantime has been immense.

Not that I think government ownership is, in itself, an answer to the problem of creating genuine equality of power in the place where most Australians experience inequality face to face: at work. There is something terribly demeaning, something *inhuman*, about the boss-worker relationship, and nationalisation often merely substitutes one form of power relationship for another. The answer, I am sure, lies with forms of organisation in which people don't simply order each other about but make decisions together, co-operatively. There is no reason why democracy shouldn't work as well on the factory floor as in politics; in England and Europe industrial democracy is being actively practised in some industries, and is being extended. The most successful forms may turn out to be complex, diverse and fairly experimental, but the principle is clear: our factories, shops, service industries, media networks and institutions should be *owned and run by the people who work there*, not by private owners and corporations. We don't need authoritarian structures in our places of work any more than we need them in our homes. Unless, of course, we really think life should be like the army.

Equality of opportunity?

I take that for granted: of course we should have equality of opportunity. And we don't. But in recent years 'equality of opportunity' has become something of a conservative catch-cry to justify grossly unequal rewards. As long as everyone starts off the same, the argument seems to go, it doesn't matter how unfairly everyone ends up. As I said before, you could justify a slave state on such grounds; everyone starts equal, the winners become emperors, the rest become slaves.

Come to think of it, maybe that's not so far from what actually does happen, in heavily disguised form, in our society; the winners in the 'race of life'—a favourite phrase among clergymen, you know, ambassadors for Jesus, who used to visit our school—become very rich and powerful, and the rest become industrial slaves. When I was in America the process was even clearer: for a start, the slaves were black. Most of them. Sometimes they revolted and burnt their ghettos down, but their political rulers, armed with things like half-tracks, tanks, tear gas and Armalite rifles, soon put the disturbances down and set up inquiries to make sure it didn't happen again. If you don't believe that this was how it was, please read my own *Up Against the Wall, America*, or Joan Didion's *The White Album*, or any account of Kent State, Attica, Jackson, Marin County, the Panthers, or the black power riots of the 1970s.

In Australia, as elsewhere, we don't even pretend to start off equal. M.J. Berry, co-editor of Davies, Encel and Berry's *Australian Society*, concluded after an exhaustive examination of the distribution of income and wealth in Australia that 'the Australian situation more closely resembles the case where a few competitors start one metre from the finishing line, a few more fifty metres back up the track, a larger group are further back hammering in their starting blocks, while the remainder are at home under the impression that the race starts tomorrow!'

Equality of opportunity is merely *what we start with*. Then we move on to other, more important equalities, the ones I've talked about. Equality of reward. Equality of power. Equality of freedom. Equality of sex, race and religion. Equality of fulfilment.

You can't guarantee the last, of course, but if every human being had the other equalities, then the chance of equality of fulfilment would be greatly enhanced. And we might get closer to the sort of human society which all of us, everywhere, deserve. As my wife's father, a lovely man and a socialist, used to say: *From each according to his ability, to each according to his need*. An old saw, but I haven't come across a better one yet.

Some people argue that if everyone was equal a great deal of the zest, the salt, would go out of life. Everyone would be the same. Well, we haven't tried it yet; why don't we give it a go and see? But anyhow, that argument confuses equality with sameness. I'm not saying everyone should be the same. There's no way in the world that could happen, given the infinite variety of human beings. Giving people equality is not going to diminish that variety; if anything, it could free people to develop their own individuality in ways which are cruelly stunted by the present system. Take something basic, like what people do with their increasingly important leisure time. Everybody has different hobbies, sports, pastimes, ways of spending their non-working lives; it's what gives human life much of its richness and diversity. But people don't have to be unequal to display that variety. You don't need kings and a leisured class to give spice to life; it's what millions of ordinary people do with their leisure, from stamp collecting to sport to orgies to reading to disco dancing (or a plenitude of mass entertainments: there is no more equal or more interesting place than a footie crowd), which provides the excitement and vivacity of mass urban culture. Socialists don't want people to be the same; they want them to be equal and free—to be different.

Well, that's it. Except for one last thing: I deliberately wrote this essay without rereading George Bernard Shaw, or Tawney, or Althusser, or any of the classic texts on equality, because I wanted to see if it were possible to write about it without making use of theory, but simply by working from first principles. I mean, it should be clear, shouldn't it, what we should do . . . maybe by just applying what used to be the old Aussie principle of 'fair go'. I reckon I worked out most of these things by the time I was a teenager. I remember sitting in the Cranbrook school dining-room once, at the trestle tables with all the other boarders, and the prefect at the head of the table, Mr King, who was also a Scout troop leader and a nice bloke, asked what I would like to do 'when I grew up'; and, thinking about those lustful fishermen and greedy wives and so on, I said I would like to do something for other people. I must have been eleven years old at the time. Ah, youthful idealism! But really, that's what this essay, and this book of essays, is about.

1982

More books

Ashbolt, Allan *An Australian Experience*, Australasian Book Society, 1974

Blesh, Rudi, *Shining Trumpets: a History of Jazz*, da Capo Press, 1948

Boggs, Carl, *Gramsci's Marxism*, Pluto Press, 1976

Cock, Peter, *Alternative Australia*, Quartet Books, 1979

Conway, Ronald, *The Great Australian Stupor*, Sun Books, 1974

Davies, A.F., Encel, Sol, & M.J. Berry (eds.), *Australian Society*, Longman Cheshire, 1977

Didion, Joan, *The White Album*, Weidenfeld & Nicolson, 1979

Eliot, T.S., *Notes Towards the Definition of Culture*, Faber, 1948

Goodman, Robert, *After the Planners*, Penguin, 1972

Gramsci, Antonio, *Prison Notebooks*, Lawrence & Wishart, 1971

Horne, Donald, Death of the Lucky Country, Penguin, 1976
  The Lucky Country, Penguin, 1964

Humphries, Barry, *A Nice Night's Entertainment*, Currency Press, 1981

Kofsky, Frank, *Black Nationalism and the Revolution in Music*, Pathfinder Press, 1970

McGregor, Craig, *The Australian People*, Hodder & Stoughton, 1980
  Don't Talk to Me about Love, Penguin, 1973
  People, Politics and Pop, Ure Smith, 1968
  Profile of Australia, Hodder & Stoughton, 1971
  Up Against the Wall, America, Angus & Robertson, 1973

MacEwen, Malcolm, *Crisis in Architecture*, R.I.B.A., 1974

Mellers, Wilfrid, *Music in a New Found Land*, Barrie & Rockliff, 1964

Moffitt, Ian *The U-Jack Society*, Ure Smith, 1972

Newton, Francis, *The Jazz Scene*, MacGibbon & Kee, 1959
Orwell, George, *Animal Farm*, Penguin, 1969
   Nineteen Eighty-Four, Penguin, 1970
Pringle, J.D. & Molnor, George, *Australian Accent*, Rigby, 1978
Spearritt, Peter & Walker, David, *Australian Popular Culture*,
   Allen & Unwin, 1979
Stretton, Hugh, *Capitalism, Socialism and the Environment*,
   Cambridge University Press (Australia) Pty Ltd, 1976
Ideas for Australian Cities, Georgian House, 1975
Tanner, Les & Coleman, Peter (eds.), *Cartoons of Australian
History*, Nelson, 1977
Vazquez, Adolfo Sancho, *Art and Society: Essays in Marxist
Aesthetics*, Merlin Press, 1977.
Walsh, Maximilian, *Poor Little Rich Country*, Penguin, 1979
Ward, Russel, *The Australian Legend*, Oxford University Press,
   1978
Waters, Edgar, in Geoffrey Dutton (ed.), *The Literature of
Australia*, Penguin, 1976
Wheelwright, E.L. & Buckley, K. (eds.), *Essays in the Political
Economy of Australian Capitalism*, 4 vols., A.N.Z., 1975—80